At the Corner of Broken & Love

Where God Meets Us in the Everyday

a memoir

Elisabeth K. Corcoran

WestBow
PRESS
A DIVISION OF THOMAS NELSON

ISBN: 978-1-4497-2260-9 (sc)
ISBN: 978-1-4497-2261-6 (e)

Library of Congress Control Number: 2011913233

WestBow Press books may be ordered through booksellers or by contacting:

WestBow Press
A Division of Thomas Nelson
1663 Liberty Drive
Bloomington, IN 47403
www.westbowpress.com
1-(866) 928-1240

Printed in the United States of America

WestBow Press rev. date: 8/2/2011

Table of Contents

Foreword

I have lived most of my adult life in partial authenticity. I have had to cover something up about myself that I didn't think anyone should know. I have lived in a very difficult marriage for over fifteen years, and other then a few close friends and whatever counselor I was seeing at the time, no one knew this about me.

My marriage reached a fever pitch the past three years, dragging me through the depths of relational hell. I have been all consumed in my thoughts with the unraveling of my marriage and it has sucked the life out of me. I have likened it to someone who has a terminal illness…I'd have good days and I'd have bad days. The bad days have found me in my pajamas, eating chocolate all day or forgetting to eat altogether. They'd find me taking one or two naps, for hours at a time. They'd find me watching too much television or sitting on my couch staring out the window with tears rolling down my cheeks. The good days, well, they'd find me putting my clothes on, sharing at a women's event, praying afterwards with a hurting woman or two, hitting the grocery store, the post office, the library, making dinner for my kids, getting them to youth group and putting them to bed with a smile and a prayer.

I assumed I had more bad days than good, but in reading over this collection of essays that I've been working on the past year, I think I must have decided somewhere along the way that I was either going to let this thing sink its hooks into me and just kill me once and for all, or I would push through. I didn't always feel like pushing through, and sometimes I didn't and there's grace for that. But in sitting down to re-read my life stories from the past year or so, I clearly chose on more than one occasion to not allow my sadness to take me down or dictate the quality of my life.

For that, I'm deeply grateful for the gift of writing. I thought this past year had been completely self-absorbed, so focused on fixing something unfixable, so pathetic and sad, that it could have just been thrown out. But as it turns out, I was still thinking deeply, still trying to sort through the other parts of my life, still trying to encourage myself and my children and my friends, still trying to change the world in tiny ways, and still, most wonderfully, looking and reaching for Jesus in all of it.

Here's the thing. This book is not about my hard marriage or its demise. (That's another book altogether.) *This* is about the rest of my life in the middle of that hard season. You see, I have been so broken the past several years, more than the average girl, I thought. But here's what I believe deep down into my bones…I'm absolutely convinced that my best life stories come from the point where my brokenness is covered over by God's love.

So enjoy a few of these stories and take courage that no matter your current life circumstances, you and God can still create beautiful stories of your own, at the corner of broken and love.

One

There's Always Next Time

Am I the only one who can ruin a perfectly good moment? It is a glorious fall day from where I sit and I decided to take another walk along a nature trail I just discovered a few days ago. It is a perfect day – probably our last good weather day in Illinois until March or so, perhaps.

When I went last time, I was completely and utterly in the moment. I was deliriously happy. Okay, for me, delirious is a quiet, satisfied smile deep down in my soul, and that's what I was. I was walking with my head thrown back, taking deep breaths, enjoying the wind in my hair, watching the leaves fall like rain, and even pretending to actually hold Jesus' hand because sometimes I do stuff like that.

Today, not so much. First, I forgot my phone. Ten years ago, whatever, right? But now I just sort of feel off when I don't have it with me. Not that I even ever talk on it. I'm one of those cell-phone-hating kind of people, but there's just something about having it with me. A security blanket, I suppose. Okay, so forgot the phone. But, moved on.

I'm walking, walking. Trying to start my deep breathing, thinking about throwing my head back a bit, when two deer are startled, from about twenty feet away from me, and run into the wetlands. Harmless deer, right? Running *away* from me. And yet, I'm now freaked out ever so slightly. I do not hold to the theory that "they are more scared of you than you are of them". I don't know where that originated, but that person should be hit over the head with a shoe. Those little deer were bigger than I am. And there were two of them. Okay, so I walked slowly, keeping my gaze fixed on them, as they were doing to me. Me realizing, that, shoot, they really blend in out there, and here I am in my orange t-shirt like a walking target. But I moved on. Or tried to.

By this time, a good three minutes into my walk, I remembered that I'm trying to work on standing up straighter so I don't end up all hunched over in my nineties and that, because of a funky little quirk in my hip, I'm being more mindful to walk with both feet pointing outward (my tendencies are to point inward, unfortunately). And why am I doing this? Because on my thirty-eighth birthday I woke up a sixty-eight-year-old with a bum hip. So, that was a preoccupation for a little bit there. Okay, moving on. Back to the moment. *Focus, Beth, focus.*

Now, I'm winding my way around in a different direction than I went the other day, so I'm in unfamiliar territory. And there is no one around. Wonderful, right? Getting away from the hustle and bustle (except my life is no longer one of hustle or bustle anymore, thankfully), but still. I should've been deeply grateful for a little bit of actual alone time on this planet. And yet, I trip over my humanity yet again and imagine being attacked. No, not by the deer this time. But by a stranger.

Now, I don't know if all girls do this. Or if I just do this from time to time. But though most of us crave even a little bit of knowing what it would feel like to be utterly alone every once in awhile, when I actually am presented with those moments, I'm then scared. And lo and behold, a Rastafarian starts walking toward me. Okay, I'm pretty sure I have not only misspelled that word, but alienated a large group of people (Rastafarians… and their friends), and shown my ignorance all in one fell swoop. So let me just say that what was walking towards me was a regular looking white man with dreadlocks. And there's nothing wrong with that. I would've been scared if I had come upon a ten-year-old girl all of the sudden in the middle of a field. Okay, so back to my little running-wild-imagination of thinking I was about to be attacked. Now I had an attacker.

Except that he kept on walking. And I kept on walking. In opposite directions. But by now, I picked up the pace just a tad, but pretended I hadn't so as not to offend. And I turned off my iPod so I could hear his footsteps behind me, just in case. And I spent the next ten minutes looking over my shoulder, all paranoid and pathetic.

Which brought me to almost being back to my car, thirty minutes later. And I said to Jesus, "I can't wait until you and I can really walk on this trail together, and I can really, actually hold your hand, and we can watch the trees come back to life and see the deer dance without fear, and I would never, and I mean not even once, look over my shoulder, because I will feel safer then I've ever been before. And because I wouldn't want to ruin that moment for anything."

Two

What Do I Want?

A friend called in tears over a long-unfullfilled dream. I feel so unsettled, she said. It's been two years, she said, and it's not getting better.

Maybe, I said, *even though this sounds scary, maybe, you need to walk deeper into it. Maybe Jesus wants you to really lay this down. Maybe he wants you to want him more than this dream*, I said.

I want many things more than I want Jesus. There are the tiny, daily, worldly, completely unjustifiable things, like a pair of red flats, just one more good hair day (because I'm apparently living one good hair day at a time these days), just one more cozy, chunky sweater to get me through this frigid, blah Illinois winter. Now, I wouldn't walk into a store and say, I need red flats...like, more than I need Jesus...in a size 7, please. But I went out today and found myself some red flats, without really thinking if I needed them...who are we kidding?...knowing I didn't need them... without asking Jesus for them. Just for an example.

And there are the big things. Good things. Worthy things that I want. I want to go to back to Africa. And fast. I want peace not just on earth but in my home, in my closest relationships. I want my third and fourth and maybe fifth books to be published.

See, good things. It's big to want to go back to Africa...that's very self-sacrificing of me. And it's good to want peace in my home, because I want my children growing up as healthy as they can. And it's worthwhile that I want my books published because I want to encourage people with my stories and point them to Jesus.

Unless, of course, I want to go back to Africa so I can tell people I've gone twice, because won't that show my commitment to social justice and that I mean business and that I must love Jesus so much to go to Africa, let alone two whole times. And maybe I want peace in my home so I can have a little more peace and love for myself. And perhaps I want my third and fourth and fifth books published because, well, the first one might just have been a fluke, and the second one was me taking the bull by the horns, and I really, really want some external validation of my worth as a person, I mean, as a writer.

But even besides all that – all the right and not-so-right things I think I want and have no idea if I need and besides all the right and not-so-right motivations behind those things, there's this lingering question that begs to be answered. That, frankly, is answered every day, all day, by each of my huge and tiny choices, that fills the slots of my mind that are marked with "now" and "today" and "urgent" and that is this: do I want Jesus more than I want anything else?

I say that I want this. And I mean it when I say it. I want to want Jesus more than anything else. But my red flats and chunky sweaters and hoping a bit too much for a publisher tell me that I don't. At least, not today.

Three

Speaking of Blessings

I speak all over Illinois. And when I say "all over", I mean within a 90-minute radius of my house. So being asked to fly out to California to speak at a mothers' group was such a treat for me. At a little church led by...well, I don't like to name-drop, so I'll just say it rhymes with Ohn Jortberg. Anyway...

The talk I was asked to give is my favorite talk. Not because it's fun to give. It's not fun to give. It's hard to give. It takes a lot out of me to give this one. It's about a few dark times in my life and it's about trying to find God through the pain. But I love it, because God shows up when I give this talk.

Now, it's one thing to give this talk ten minutes from my house; it's a whole other story to fly across the country to give this talk. It felt weightier. It felt...and I say this humbly...important. Like, of the one hundred and twenty women in that room, someone (or more than one someone) had an appointment with God for some healing.

My list of prayer requests was as long as my arm, from sleeping well the night before I left, to figuring out how to get to the parking lot and then to the gate all by myself for the first time, to being filled with the Spirit and having a great hair day. (Yes, I pray for stuff like that. It doesn't always come to pass, but I pray for it all.)

Every request of mine was answered. And then I got some bonuses.

I had a delicious dinner with two very sweet ladies.

I was put up in an adorable bed & breakfast, and didn't waste my time by watching television (this is huge for me).

I got to go for a run on a beautiful, February, California, non-gray-Illinois morning.

Jesus led me to a couple Scriptures so intimately during my devotions that I struggled between awe and almost nonchalance because I'm getting used to him doing that for me.

The first part of the event was simply beautiful – an authentic testimony, engaging worship, and mutual sharing of Scriptures that had me on the verge of tears before I took my place on stage.

I got to pray with a woman afterwards who just walked up to my book table and started to cry. She came behind the table, bent down, and I put my arms around her, stroking her hair and praying for her the way I think Jesus would have. (And you know what? If the only reason I spent 24 hours going to California and back was to show compassion to that one woman, touch her gently, and pray with her…than that was enough for me.)

I felt part of something bigger than me. I felt like one piece of a jigsaw puzzle that would hopefully do good well after I flew home.

One last unexpected blessing…on the way home on the plane, looking over the sun setting over the mountains, I started to thank Jesus for letting me do this, for setting this up for me, and I felt him say to me, before I could get to it, "You did good, baby. Thank you for obeying Me and following Me out here." And I told him, I wouldn't have missed it for the world.

Four

Up the Mountain, Down the Mountain

I used to think the elusive spiritual mountaintop experience was the goal. Even if it consisted of only a few fleeting moments. I wanted to live on the mountain. I had visions that heaven would be like the mountaintop.

But something happened recently that is forcing me to rethink that theory. I have had a ridiculously long string of hard life situations...like year after year. I am not complaining, as you'll see in a moment. But I've definitely learned to live in difficulty. In fact, I just said to a friend yesterday, "I'm used to living miserably in Christ...in fact, I'm fabulous at it!"

But then something shifted. Slightly enough that it would not be noticed by the casual observer, but huge enough that it broke something wide open in me. I feel...ummm, how do I say this...healed. Okay, healing. And though that is an amazing thing...something I've been praying for and longing for...for years...now that it's here, I don't know what to do with myself.

To the same friend I said, "I don't think I know how to celebrate in Christ. How to be joyful in Jesus. How to be happy, period." (But I'm working on it.)

Because when I am in crisis, when I am struggling, when I am desperate...the thing I'm desperate for is God and more and more of Him alone. But when all things are well in my little world (or at least more well than they've been in a long time) and circumstantial peace is what is surrounding me, I'm befuddled. I'm lost. It's like I'm only content in crisis. Like drama is what runs through my veins and keeps my heart pumping. And keeps me front and center in the throne room of God.

Just this morning, as I sat on a bench outside with a cup of tea, looking out at my pond as the sun came up, with birds starting their day…I said to no one in particular, or maybe to Jesus himself, "I want the hard times closeness even though it's peaceful."

So I think, for me, the mountaintop is the hard climb up through trials, moving me closer and closer to God…it's where I want to be because I'm interwoven with him in a way I'm not in the easy places.

If trials ready us for our face-to-face encounter with Christ, and if they are what move us into his presence deeper than ease, then I want the hard times. I may sound crazy, but I seriously do. Because it's been about ten days of this peace, and, really, I already miss Jesus.

Five

Habit or Hope?

One of our cats has been missing for five days. It's been sad and we've been coming to terms with the loss (my kids more than me, but me more than I ever thought).

My daughter has had this daily custom of calling them as soon as she steps off the bus at the end of the day. If you meander, it's about a two minute stroll down our driveway, and she belts out in a sing-song-y voice, "Oscar, Rosie…Oscar, Rosie…" and they follow suit by coming running to greet her. I've never seen cats do this. Rosie, the girl, is very nonchalant. She'll walk up to Sara, rub up against her leg and walk away, as if to say, "Yes, I see you're home. What's in it for me?" Oscar on the other hand, will fall down in front of her on his side, imploring, "Please, please give me some love." And then he lets Sara pet him for minutes at a time.

Well, yesterday, four days into Oscar being gone, Sara stepped off the bus, and commenced her routine…"Oscar, Rosie…Oscar, Rosie…". Rosie came. Oscar, of course, did not. I was sitting outside waiting for her and thought to myself, "Habit or hope?"

Which got me thinking, how much of my life do I do out of habit or hope? I'm not even going to do any commentating on whether it's good or bad. Or if there's another reason to do something. If there should be another reason. I get up in the morning out of habit. I also must have some hope that life is not going to crash around me the moment my feet hit the floor. I go for a run out of habit. Also out of the hope that it will give me a bit more energy later in the day, somehow. I spend time with Jesus out of habit. But also out of the hope that he will change my clunky heart, even if just a little bit.

So I guess it's not either/or. It sounds like it's a bit of both, along with motives buried deep that even I cannot figure out.

An incredible postscript…I just went to put a letter in the mailbox, and did the Sara sing-song-y "Oscar, Rosie" call…definitely out of hope… feeling foolish…feeling like a little girl who still believes in miracles…and a very wet, very hungry and tired looking Oscar appeared like an oasis. Oh, will Sara be ecstatic when she gets off the bus today.

Six

My Girl

Today I had one role: Sara's mom. I didn't write (until right now). I didn't clean or do laundry (not a huge sacrifice). I just did a few things that moms have to do from time to time. She had a small medical procedure that required sleep deprivation. Well, any mom knows that if the kid has to be sleep deprived, so does the mom. So I got up with her at 4am and we watched "The Incredibles". Why not, really? I made her breakfast at about 5. Had her take a shower at 6 to stay awake. I had my devotions, took a shower and we headed out by 8:30. We sat around a waiting room for an hour and a half, playing I Spy and making totally inappropriate, sleep-deprived, floopy comments about our surroundings, as one can do with an almost-teenager.

And then we went in for the procedure. A simple EEG that left her strapped to twenty-two wires, lying in a Lazy Boy, needing to keep her eyes closed for almost an hour. The room was dark and I had nowhere to go and nothing to do but look at my daughter.

When was the last time I just looked at her? Let alone to simply marvel? Because she really is a beauty, that one. She doesn't know it yet. In fact, she might just totally doubt it. About her outer and her inner beauty. But I see it.

She is a delight to me. And I say this knowing a couple things. One, at times we drive each other absolutely crazy (and that's okay). Two, she is so much like me it's scary. And three, I think she is so much like me because I am who she sees…but there's so, so much more to her than just being my copy. She, simultaneously, is so different from me as well.

Thankfully, she's better than me. A better version. And hopefully, oh Jesus, please hopefully, her foundation will be just a tad firmer, already starting her life out in His hands.

She's almost thirteen. I remember almost thirteen. I hated almost thirteen. She seems to be balancing it pretty well from my vantage point, even if she doesn't think so. There is still a part of her that is so…I was going to say 7 or 8…but it's not a certain age…just still little girl. Still holds my hand, when no one is around. And yet, sometimes when they are. Still whines at the slightest hint of a chore. Still runs into her daddy's arms. Still panics over the thought of a shot. But then there's the grown-up inside. The girl with the whip-smart wit that I can totally banter back and forth with, forgetting sometimes that she's only twelve. The part of her that makes dinner for us. (Didn't see that perk coming…would've had her ages ago.) The part of her who decides on a whim to start a business making and selling bracelets, so she can give all the money to Africa. And the part of her who starts writing a book, about two teenage girls who go to Uganda and their lives complete change. She's writing a book. It's really good. She's twelve.

So today was about Sara. And about stopping to look at her. To watch her. To really think about who she is right now. To ask Jesus to give her big adventures. To ask him to remind her she is so completely loved that she doesn't have to run out and make a million big and little mistakes trying to find love somewhere else.

I can't believe I get to be her mom.

Seven

Can't Undo It

In thinking through some of the things that our world has been through, in feeling the weight of my ancestors' choices, choices that I had nothing to do with but still feel responsible for, I have been saddened and ashamed.

I've been wondering what I would've done in their shoes. What in the world can I possibly do now to make up for what someone else did?

But this also makes me think of all the things I've done wrong. So many poor choices. Things I would give anything to undo, knowing I will never have the chance.

But then the beautiful phrase *living amends* comes to mind. It's the concept that not only do you apologize for what you've done, but you attempt to make up for it by changing your thoughts and attitudes, your words and actions toward the person you hurt in all future interactions.

I think of the well-known serenity prayer and how I have come to not just pray it from time to time, but I've used it when sifting through my jaded emotions, my relational misfires.

God, grant me the serenity, the peace, to accept the things I cannot change...

I cannot change one moment of my past.

I cannot change one moment of the world's history.

I cannot change what I did yesterday.

I cannot change what my great-great-great-grandfather may have chosen to do, good or bad, and how that trickled down through the generations.

I cannot change what someone has done to me or thinks about me. No matter what I do.

...the courage to change the things I can...

Here's where I make my next steps list, basically.

I cannot change the decisions I made that led me to my here and now, but I can make sure that I am grateful for where it led me.

I cannot change the genocides that have taken place, for instance, but I can pray and give and go and influence.

I cannot change how I hurt someone, perhaps over and over again. But I can do my best to speak more kindly to them in the future, even giving them space and time to heal if need be.

I cannot change that my family, way back in history, may have owned slaves. But I can fight against racism in thought and word and deed.

I cannot change the hurt that I've felt, even recently, but I can pray for healing and pray for the bravery to be gentle in the midst of pain.

Living amends. Using my life to fix what's been done in the past. Using the light that Jesus says I have in me to obliterate the darkness that has filled my past, our past, for a future that falls, hopefully, more along Kingdom lines. *Lord, give me the courage...*

Be gentle, even in the midst of pain.
It's not natural. It's just plain brave.

Eight

Tell Me All Your Feelings

I have an eleven-year-old son which, for some reason, immediately conjures up the phrase *no man's land*. There's just something about an eleven-year-old boy that seems so in-between. He wants to be a man, he wants to play football, he wants me to teach him how to drive in parking lots. And yet, he's scared to start middle school (okay, I don't care what age you are, any one would be scared to start middle school), he still tenderly holds my hand when we're alone, and he doesn't know what to do with his feelings.

The other day we were driving around and I asked him about school starting...*how do you feel about it, bud? Not good*, he said. *What about it is not good*, I asked. *I don't know*, he replied.

Okay then. Glad we had this heart to heart, I'm thinking.

This all-too-familiar exchange with him...me asking questions, him answering in less than a handful of monosyllabic words...made me think back to something a guy friend said to me years ago. I was asking him what he felt about something and he said, without batting an eye and in all honesty, "If I ever figure out what I feel about something, I'll tell you."

I have never forgotten that one line. Probably because I couldn't relate in the least. I'm the kind of girl who knows what I'm feeling. I'm the kind of girl who can name what I'm feeling, even if it's seventeen feelings all at once. And I can tell you to what degree and in order of priority. I'm the kind of girl who journals about her feelings and, for the most part, knows how to express them. Whether anyone else in my immediate world wants me to or not. I get feelings. I love feelings.

As a mom, I believe it's my responsibility to send my kids out into the world knowing what they feel about something and how to express it in a healthy way. To realize that my son, if left to his own devices, would grow up like my guy friend and have no idea what he is ever feeling, let alone how to express it, was just unacceptable to me.

So when we got home, I sat down at my computer and wrote up a list of six common feelings, along with their definitions, a list of synonyms, how to know when that's what you're feeling, and how to express that feeling in a healthy way. And that list was our bedtime story that night. It went so well, that he even asked me to "go over that one again" because I apparently struck a chord with one of them. That list is taped next to his bed. That list, I hope, is just the beginning of many good conversations as I prepare my son for the world.

And, future daughter-in-law, you're very welcome.

Nine

Moving a Few Mountains & Conquering Some Graves

"Saviour, He can move the mountains,
    My God is mighty to save,
    He is mighty to save.
    Forever, Author of salvation,
    He rose and conquered the grave,
    Jesus conquered the grave."

This song was on the radio this morning as I was returning from my run. I was singing along, nothing so unusual. I pulled into my garage, I got to the chorus, and by the time I reached "Jesus conquered the grave", I was crying uncontrollably with my hands gripping the steering wheel.

I know, that's not the makings of a convincing song review on iTunes.

But I was struggling with something this morning. A very frustrating conversation I had on the phone on the way to my run. A conversation that made me want to throw my phone out the window. But I didn't. A conversation that helped me run a bit faster than I usually do because I was so filled with ticked-off-inspired adrenaline. I do enjoy those kinds of runs.

So back to the garage crying. I turned off the car and said, "Jesus, please conquer my grave." He knows the thing that's weighing me down. He knows the thing that breaks my heart. He knows how that stupid little phone conversation was about so much more than what was said on the phone. He knows the burden I'm carrying, better than I even do. So I asked him to move this mountain of mine and to conquer this grave.

And then I wiped away my tears and walked back into my house, quietly singing the song the rest of the morning. And I wait.

Ten

Checking Motives, Letting Go & Shutting Up

Two percent.

No, I'm not talking about my milk preference. I'm talking about the part of the hard conversation that I tend to keep to myself even if it really needs to be put out there.

I had a relational thing a little while ago that is as wrapped up as it can be. It was one of those messy things that you totally wish you could undo. I'm picturing a suitcase being opened, innocently, only to have mounds of clothing and jewelry unsuspectingly come flying out, and then me sitting on it trying to stuff everything back in. Trying to undo what cannot be undone. This relational thing was kind of like that.

But, like I said, it's done. Ish. Because I've got that two percent lurking in my mind. I'll be sitting at my computer or a stoplight and a memory of the whole yucky thing will just interrupt my perfectly fine day and I'll remember that there's two percent more I want to say, that things just aren't right and there feels like there's nothing I can do about it but let time go by.

I asked a dear friend for her advice on what I should do about those lingering thoughts and here's what she said:

"I tend to write out that two percent and hold it for awhile. If it will help me and hurt no one, I usually send it. Sometimes I regret the response and consequences...sometimes it's good. I don't think it has ever been great. While in the holding pattern, seek the Holy Spirit. I'm finding most things don't matter nearly as much to others as they matter to me. If you give it to Jesus alone...let it go....let him work. Then go bless someone else."

I especially loved the line: "I'm finding most things don't matter nearly as much to others as they matter to me."

Isn't this so true?

I could be mulling this over...okay, let's call it what it is...obsessing about getting my last little two cents in there...and first of all, it could totally do more damage...rip off the scab that's trying to heal, or secondly, the other person could be like, what are you even talking about?

So I took her sound advice. I wrote out that two percent. I handed it to Jesus. I asked if I should say it and now I am waiting for guidance. I'll probably just let it go, especially because more than likely, this is way more about me than the greater good of us then I'm willing to admit.

And if I'm letting myself learn anything over time it's that the greater good is far more important to me than just my little wants and needs.

Eleven

Gone Before

I've found comfort recently in a worship song entitled "I Will Go Before" which simply means that Jesus is just up ahead of me, in all things. But just this morning it dawned on me that not only will he go before me, but that he already has gone before me.

Jesus is above time. When I say those words I can't help but picture a panoramic view of a stage, with marionettes and the puppeteer up above being able to see all the action going on at once. Please don't get bogged down in this analogy...I am not implying that God is the Master Puppeteer, just yanking us around on strings and we have no say in anything. Though I fully believe he knows every single thing that has happened, is happening and is going to happen, I also simultaneously and fully believe that we have free will. (My proof: I've messed up way too much in my life to blame God for controlling my actions. All those mistakes, all those sins, one hundred percent me.)

I think I focus most of my comprehension of Jesus as the Alpha and the Omega, the Beginning and the End. He is where I started and he is where I will end up. But he is also the Author of my faith. Author, to me, implies a writer. Someone who is currently writing something. My life is the current thing that is being written.

So though he will go before me, and I am so glad, he already has gone before me. Which means that he doesn't just know my end. He knows what will happen between now and my end. He knows my in the meantime. He holds my end in his hands, yes. But he holds every other moment in between. My next ten actions. My next hundred sins; and hopefully, my next hundred sorry's. My next thousand tries to do better next time. My next million thoughts. My next billion reasons to celebrate and be grateful. He holds it all. He sees it all. He has gone before it all.

And on a hard morning, knowing that not a thing...not one single thing...can come my way that hasn't been first quality-control-checked by my Heavenly Father brings sweet relief and deep comfort.

Twelve

Cower No More

I had a little thing with a couple of people at church recently. "A little thing" is the most I'm going to say about it. I said something that I felt led to say and I handled it the way I sometimes tend to handle relational things...not all that well...and it was received as relational things sometimes tend to be received, when I'm involved, at least...not all that well. I'm not sure what I was expecting. Actually, I hadn't thought that far. I was just following some marching orders.

But since then, I've been, ummm, uncomfortable at church. Each week has left me with thoughts like, should I sit in a different spot? Will there be eye contact this week? Will there be a hello? A hug maybe?

This week was no different. I came in and tentatively found a seat. I was thinking mid-service how I wished I could get my kids, invisibly, like Violet from "The Incredibles", and get to my car without being noticed.

But right around then, Jesus said to me, "Did you do what I had told you to do?" I said, "Yes." And he responded, "Then stop cowering."

Yes, sir.

So I stopped. When the service was over, I didn't worry about eye contact (there was none) or words (there were none). But I did go on to have five (yes, I just counted) casual encounters with people and two fairly significant ones that I would not have had if I had just slunk out and quickly got my kids.

I don't know how much longer this thing is going to be hanging around, but as far as I'm concerned, I've done all I've can, I'm done second-guessing, they know I love them and they know I'm sorry, (they may be long over it and I'm just obsessing...), and I'm not cowering any more.

Thirteen

In Their Meantimes

I met with two of my closest friends, separately, within a half hour of each other. Both cried. Though I was the common denominator, it thankfully wasn't something I said. One is waiting on something that she's not sure will ever come to pass, an unsatisfied, deep soul longing. One is in the midst of about sixteen crappy things. Pardon the use of *crappy*. And the slight exaggeration of sixteen, though it probably feels like sixteen to her.

And I recently saw someone, when asked how she was, said, "Home is sucky. Work is sucky." So sad. Too sad.

My heart hurts for each of these women. There's not much I can do. Pray for. Pray with. Try to lighten the mood for a minute or two by saying something slightly inappropriate in the hopes of getting a smile through the tears. Send a card. Suggest a book maybe, or a Psalm or two. Offer up a few thoughts. Hold a hand. Affirm. Remind.

Remind as in, it's all going to be alright. Really. Big picture. It's all going to eventually be all right.

But my desire to get in there and fix things, or to even get in there and take it all away, cannot be acted upon.

These aren't human things. I can't fix these things even if it were the right thing to do. Sure, there are probably a couple things they can do in their meantimes, things they are probably each doing and trying, but most of it all is waiting on God to move. Not that he's not moving. So maybe better put is waiting on the clarity to see how God's moving even in the quiet, even in the pain, even in the trials, even in the crisis, even in the hard.

In a way, I can wait with them. That's part of friendship. But in another sense, I walk away, knowing I can only do so much, and remind myself… it's all going to be all right…it's all going to be all right…eventually, it really is.

Fourteen

Finish That Thing Already

I am working on memorizing Scripture. Don't pat me on the back, I'm only on day three. Here's what I've got so far.

James 1: 2-4a

Consider it pure joy, my brothers, when you face trials of many kinds, because you know that the testing of your faith develops perseverance. Perseverance must finish its work...

(YES! Just did that without looking.)

But here's where it goes from my head and deep down into my heart and soul.

I will have trials. Life has been, currently is, and will continue to be difficult and full of challenges and sadnesses. (Though, yes, it can be and is very, very good and can be and is full of many, many wonderful gifts. But that's not what this passage is about...)

But I am to be joyful and even grateful when looking down the barrel of yet another hardship, when standing at the bottom of another mountain-sized obstacle, when sitting with or fighting against another tearful heartbreak.

Why? Because I know what any given trial is really all about. It's not about the trial itself. It's about what comes from and after, hopefully, gracefully and faithfully walking through it.

And that is a strength that matures me, a strength that shapes me a little bit more into the image of Christ.

And good times, though blessings and soul-restoring in and of themselves, do not make me more like Jesus. Only trials can do that.

I know from first-hand experience that my darkest moments have defined my faith and have led me to my deepest stretches of growth. And I also know that when all is relatively well in my little world (which, by the way, should not be the goal of any Christ-follower), I skate through with no real need to depend on Jesus moment to moment.

I understand the penchant for trying to avoid pain, don't get me wrong. I've even been known to ask Jesus for the intimacy minus the necessary hardship…recently. (Turns out, he doesn't roll that way.)

But, bottomline, life is hard. And difficulties = Christ forming in me (when I don't fight it).

So I'll take a little more of Jesus while going through the fire over easy street on my own any day of the week.

And I'll say it again: I'll consider it pure joy, my brothers and sisters, whenever I face trials of many kinds, because I know that the testing of my faith develops perseverance. And I desperately want perseverance to finish its work in me.

Fifteen

Free to Just Be

One way I know that God loves me was a sweet gift he gave me last year. When I asked him if I could quit my job, he not only said yes, I felt him tell me that he would fill my days with rest and purpose if I let him. I had always, deep down, felt that he'd really only love me if I really served him like crazy, even to the point of exhaustion…that was, like, the Christian thing to do. So telling me I could quit, well, that was Love.

Today, I just had another moment. I was having my daily time with Jesus. I'm not staunch with this when it comes to others, just myself. And maybe my kids. And the only reason I'm disciplined with it is because I know how much I need it. Thankfully, I'm in a sweet season where it doesn't feel like a waste of time or one more thing on my to-do list (though I do write it on my to-do list) or just another Christian-should. But today, something happened during my quiet time that has never happened to me before in all of my years of quiet times, best as I can recall.

I fell asleep.

No big deal, right? People fall asleep praying at night before bed all the time. Ummm, this was at 8:30. In the morning. Granted, my body must not be used to the new getting-up schedule of 5:15. But still. Really? A nap at 8:30? Let alone while I was DOING SOMETHING…and another let alone…SOMETHING AS IMPORTANT AS TALKING TO THE CREATOR OF THE WORLD. Just dozed off for a bit there.

But I almost couldn't help myself. It wasn't even that I was that exhausted, I don't think. It was a combination of the sun warming up my face on the spot I sit on my couch, coupled with the just-perfect-enough breeze blowing in through the open window on this gorgeous morning. But it was one more thing too.

I felt free. Completely free in God's presence. I knew I could lay my head down, and pull that blanket up, and close my eyes, still feeling the sun and the breeze. Still considering this to be time with Jesus. I knew he wasn't up there rolling his eyes at me or all ticked off at my lack of discipline. In fact, when I woke up, I wrote, "Just fell asleep. Sorry, Jesus. And yet…I feel more loved than I've felt in a long time."

There's a freedom that comes in a relationship that is well-worn. In a coupling that sometimes doesn't need words to express what's really going on. That doesn't even need to be expressing something in the first place at every given moment. He knows me. Like, really, really knows me. Better than I know me. And I know him. And today's time with Jesus was about taking a nap with him and not much else. And knowing that was more than okay.

So, my question to you is, how free do you feel?

Sixteen

Split Open

I love words. And there are times, when I read a quote that I've never seen before, and it just grabs me, and I wish I had written it. I've even wondered how only a few words, put together just so, can have such power. And how no one had ever thought to put that particular combination together before.

This was one of those quotes for me:

"What would happen if one woman told the truth about her life? The world would be split open." Muriel Rukeyser

Seriously. What would happen?

We all hide. (And if you say you don't, you're not telling the truth about your life.) We're all hiding from each other, from ourselves, from God. But what if we stopped the hiding and the pretending and just said what really needs to be said, just said those words that hurt coming out of our throats. Those words that paint the picture of what's really going on in our hearts. The ones that cause us, and sometimes others, to have tears roll down our cheeks that we can't brush away fast enough.

I'm working on this. Okay, my closest friends would say I've been working on this and I've got it nailed. I tend to tell the truth. The ugly truth. The more-than-you-may-have-wanted-to-know truth.

But I look at it this way. If we're all just trying to get through life, figuring it out the best that we can, and I act like I've got it all together, and you act like all your ducks are in a row, and she acts like nothing's wrong, and he acts like how could anything be better...then who are we helping? (And who are we kidding?)

Because the truth is that my life is a difficult thing from time to time. Sometimes, it's much more difficult that I ever would have signed up for. And if all I do is put on my make-up and make sure each hair is in place and my outfit not only matches but is trendy and I walk up to you and answer with a hearty "fine" to your "how are you?" and keep going, I've done you a terrible disservice. Because you just might be hurting too. And maybe if I told the truth and answered, even once, "not so great…how about you?", something could actually split open, like your heart or your thoughts or your life or your world, and you could see that you're not alone and we could walk that road together for awhile, and you know what? It would be beautiful. In fact, it would be magnificent.

Because I'll take truth and hard and beauty over fake and just fine and blah every single time.

Seventeen

Really? All We Need is...

Why I didn't start my new memorizing kick with my favorite passage is beyond me, because I *love* these words.

Zephaniah 3:17
The Lord your God is with you,
He is mighty to save.
He will take great delight in you,
He will quiet you with his love,
He will rejoice over you with singing.

I'm sorry, but seriously?

What would my life look like if I really believed each of these five amazing promises? I bet a good 95% of my problems would just disappear. If I connected these statements to my life...if you connected these words to your life...just think about it...

If I really believed that the Lord my God is with me, right now, this moment, in every single circumstance? I'd be lighter. I'd be without worry, without stress, without anxious thoughts. If I really believed it.

If I really believed that my God is mighty to save? Not just in terms of my actual salvation, but to save me from myself...to save me from the situation that feels like it's just about to swallow me alive, to save me from the relationship issues that haunt me? I'd hand over every single burden and care the moment it came to mind, and then I'd be free to keep walking. If I really believed it.

If I really believed that my God takes delight in me? And not just delight...he's not just, you know, mildly amused by me...the God of the universe takes great delight in who I am as his beloved, as his creation.

Get out of town. Talk about being so filled up that I can love others with abandon. If I really believed it.

If I really believed that my God could quiet me with his love? Could shut out the racing thoughts and the overwhelming worries and the horribly insecure thoughts about my lack of worth simply with his deep, abiding, loyal, cuts-through-everything Love. Oh, my soul melts at this one... Think of how peaceful I'd be. Think of how quietly, humbly confident I'd be. Think about how I'd never have to judge or criticize another human being because I would be quieted deep down by Love. If I really believed it.

And what if I really believed that my God is rejoicing over me with a song? That he is looking at me right now, thinking about me with a smile on his holy face, remembering the joy he took in creating me just so, and he's so moved, that he starts humming, maybe whistling a little bit, only to break out in a song of rejoicing...over me. Over you. I can barely take it in. I know I'm supposed to praise and worship my God and my King, but really...he adores me enough to sing a song over me? How I would rest... how I could stop all the running and trying so hard. If I really believed.

What joy...I am starting to believe. Finally, this late in the game... this far along in my walk with him...I'm starting to let these Truths with a capital T sink in to my heart and soul. What would your life look like if you really believed all of this about yourself? Just try it...and then watch, even if just for today, about 95% of your problems wash away.

Eighteen

Anti-thesis to Hiding

A few days ago I wrote about speaking the truth and what that could do to this world and for each other.

But just a couple nights ago, I had some irony smack me gently in the face.

I'm in a new small group, new to me, with about eight other women. Half of them I've known for ten to fifteen years, a few others maybe two or three, one gal I just met. At the beginning check-in time, everyone said something that was going on…a concern or praise in their life…but when it came to me, all I had was, while laughing, "I've got a cold…" So benign was my little tidbit that the gal next to me didn't even write my name down to pray for me this week (I don't blame her and actually think it's kind of funny).

Later when we broke up into pairs to pray, the gal I was with said, "So, it sounds like things are great with you?" She wasn't being sarcastic. I have, in the past three weeks, led this group to believe that I'm leading an intentionally slow-paced life, doing only what I love to do, not a care in the world, except, of course, for my sniffles.

Hmmm. So, is everything really great with me? And if not, am I giving that false impression that will only be a disservice to others like I was talking about?

Well, yes and no.

Everything is well with my soul. Very well, actually. So on that front, yes, I am great.

But not everything is well with my circumstances. I know what you may be thinking…but, Beth, all you said the other day when asked how

35

your life is is that you have a cold. Way to be authentic. Way to actually do what you write about.

Okay, okay, hear me out. I don't know all of these women well. This new small group is not my inner circle. My inner circle, well, they know the ins and outs of my circumstances. And my soul, for that matter.

So I guess I need to clarify. Though I am a proponent of authenticity or what's the point, I believe fully in choosing wisely - after years of messing up on this - when and where and what I share about my heart and all its gory details. Not everyone needs to know everything about my life.

So to those people, the ones who will more than likely never know the full-on truth in all its glory, know this...you may not hear the particulars coming out of my mouth, but I promise to never let you think, as far as it is up to me, that you are alone in whatever it is you're going through. Because odds are I've either been through it, or something similar, or possibly still am. Even if I don't say it.

And that's my truth.

Nineteen

Thank You for Not Smoking

A favorite Bible teacher of mine, Beth Moore, did a bit on Shadrach, Meshach, and Abednego when doing her Daniel series. In one of her sessions she made a point of relating their experience being tossed into the fiery furnace with fiery trials in our lives, saying that when they came out, they didn't even smell like smoke. She went on to say that some people, when going through a hard time, smell a whole lot like smoke. Everybody knows the troubles they've seen, because they're telling ever-y-body.

I have smelled like smoke. For a long time. I've got one particular trouble that, though the entire world does not know about it, my inner circle knows about, and has, for years. And, probably more details than they even wish but they're too sweet to tell me that.

But when I was watching this video session, tears began to stream down my face and I said outloud, to no one but myself and Jesus, I don't think I smell like smoke anymore.

I've still got the thing. My furnace is still fiery, and I'm still standing in it, but it's not burning as brightly and I'm not telling all passers-by about the number of coals and the temperature of the flame and my lack of drinking water and such.

Know why? Because I've received help. Because I've finally tapped into the presence of Christ standing in that fiery trial with me. Because, gasp, people can change. And, yes, truly, God does in fact still heal.

The woman who I see in the mirror these days doesn't need to tell everybody her troubles because her troubles aren't defining her anymore. And because she is shrinking the influence that this stickler has in her life. And because she is healing.

Not healed, mind you. This'll be a lifetime process. But healing for sure. In fits and starts some days, but in leaps and bounds it feels like on some others. Healing enough that I can give a little bit of it away. Healing enough that I am able to look back and see all the good that has been coming out of that fiery trial. Healing enough that I don't smell like smoke anymore.

And healing enough that I can withstand staying put for the time being because I see the big picture and all the glory that will come. And boy, will there be glory.

Twenty

As Close as I Can Get

Psalm 73:28
But as for me, it is good to be near God.
I have made the Sovereign Lord my refuge.
I will tell of all His deeds.

This verse feels like a gentle breeze on a just-warm-enough day with a cup of tea in my hand. This verse wraps around me. Like a blanket. Like protection. Like love.

But as for me. I can only speak for myself. And after years of walking with Christ, this is one thing that I am confident in saying.

It is good, more than good, for me to be near God. As near as I can. So close I hear the whispers. So next-to that the shadow of his wing is my covering.

I have made. I have chosen. I have been intentional. I have come to him time and time again. He has been my first thing, my best thing. Not as much as I wish, but it's becoming more so every day.

The Sovereign Lord. Who's in control? Surely not me. Who knows every thing? Only One can. Who is all-powerful? My Sovereign Lord. Why wouldn't I want to depend on him?

My refuge. I sink into these words. I let this phrase surround me. I picture a cleft in a rock by a stream and a large, old tree for shade. I can hunker down here. I can be refreshed here. I am safe here.

I will tell. I need to speak, use my words, express what I feel deep down inside. I can't keep it inside, and I don't want to.

Of all his deeds. There are so many. Volumes and volumes. And that's just what he's done in my life. So much good he has done.

So as for me, I'm going to get as close as I can to my good, all-knowing God, and let his love enfold around me, hem me in, and shelter me.

Twenty One

Mind the Gap

For God did not give us a spirit of fear,
but a spirit of power, of love, and of a sound mind.
We have the mind of Christ.
2 Timothy 1:7 & 1 Corinthians 2:16b

It's been brought to my attention as of late that I've been forgetting key components of key conversations. It's happened enough that it's been named. I have, apparently, some *gaps*.

When this was first brought up, I have to admit that I dismissed it, thinking this person was simply deflecting from the meat of whatever topic we were on. But when it was brought up again, it seems the only thing this person wanted from me was admission that this in actuality could be true…that I could have gaps.

Well, I said, *if I do have gaps, would I even remember having them?*

I was trying to be funny. We did both laugh a bit. But I did have to confess that anything really is possible. I could very well be having mind gaps. I'm getting older. So, memory tends to slip, I suppose. Plus, I've never prided myself on having a mind like a steel trap. I could also argue that I tend to remember things that are important to me, and let slip things that maybe are not so.

All that to say, I simply asked Jesus to strengthen my memory. To make this a non-issue so it wouldn't become any more of a relational stumbling block than it was becoming.

And do you know what he did? (And, I have to give credit to my dear friend, Charlotte, for even pointing this out to me, because I had not connected the dots at all on this one.) But this is what he did. (And I need to tell a roundabout story to get to my point.)

About a month before school started, I got it in my head that I should start memorizing Scripture with my kids. But by the time I gathered some advice from other seasoned moms on how to do this, school was starting and I didn't want to add to my kids' burden of homework and new classes and teachers and friends and football and youth group by telling them they also had to try to remember the book of Philippians or something. So, I decided to give it some time before bringing up the idea to Sara and Jack.

But that didn't mean I couldn't start with myself. So, sometime during the first week of school, I started reading in the book of James and began with a small passage to memorize. You must understand something. I have never made Scripture memory a priority before, in all my years of walking with Christ. Mainly out of laziness but I also just thought it would be too hard and I wouldn't be able to do it.

I'm not going to say how many I've memorized so far, because that's not the point, but what I will say is that I have been memorizing verses in the past three or so weeks with an ease that I didn't know existed.

I shudder to even write this, thinking a) the enemy will read this and jump all over it and I'll not only not be able to memorize anymore, but he'll somehow make me forget the ones I have memorized…and b) yikes, what might God be preparing me for that He's allowing me to memorize like this? (I hate that I think like this.)

But here's where Charlotte's insight comes in. She said to me the other morning something like, "How precious of God to allow you to memorize so easily at a time when you're questioning the soundness of your mind. It's as if he's telling you that your mind and memory are more than fine…"

I teared up immediately when she said that. It hadn't even occurred to me, but, yes, how like my God to answer a prayer in a way I couldn't even have imagined.

Twenty Two

Slice of Heaven - Part One of Three

I've been meaning to write about Heaven and how to get there ever since hearing a message by my pastor where he pointed out that people may see Christ in us because of our works but they will only be able to enter into a relationship with Him with the help of our words.

So, here goes.

I believe that Jesus is God's only Son, and that he died on the cross for my sin. I believe that Jesus did not just die for the generic sin of the world, but for my specific mountain of sin. I believe that you must ask him for forgiveness and to lead your life to enter into a saving relationship with him. I believe that this not only leads to eternity with God in Heaven but a fulfilling life on earth as it taps into the most important part of a human being, the soul. He meets needs in me that no thing or person can fill. And I cannot imagine my life without him.

I am looking forward to eternity with him, especially the closer I become to him, but I am beyond grateful as is for his companionship on the journey of this life.

And this is a sample prayer of what you can say when you realize you don't yet have a personal relationship with God but you want one.

Dear God, I come to you now to tell you that I believe you exist. That the Bible is true. That Jesus is your Son and that he died on the cross. Not just for the collective sins of the world, but for my sins...all I've ever committed and all I'll ever commit. I am sorry for all the things I've ever done to hurt you and for not seeking you sooner. I am thankful that you allowed Christ to die for me. I accept the free gift of salvation and ask that you will live in me and lead my life from now on. Help me to know you, to love you, to trust you, to obey you and to follow you. Amen.

Twenty Three

Helluva Bad Time – Part Two of Three

There's a lovely little movie coming out this month called "I Hope They Serve Beer in Hell". I think it won a couple awards at Sundance for its depth and cinematography. (Read: dripping sarcasm)

If someone is actually hoping this - that their favorite alcoholic beverages will be served in their self-assumed destination - they are sorely mistaken.

I am sick and tired of hearing people refer to Hell as a never-ending party where they'll get to spend forever with their best buds, drinking and getting high and various other things that tickle their fancy.

You know who's not sick and tired of this perception of Hell? Satan. Nope, he is thrilled beyond words if he can snow anyone into thinking that Hell will be fun, that Hell is where your friends are going so why wouldn't you want to go there too?

Not to be all Debbie Downer, but let me tell you what Hell will be like. Granted, I've never been there. But my source is the Bible. And I believe the Bible to be true. Not just because I live in la-la land and not because I don't have two brain cells to rub together. This book has not only stood the test of time, but it's been proved true by archaeological and historical evidence. Plus, God has done so much for me personally that I cannot not believe. Anyway, back to Hell.

I'm getting these statements from author, Randy Alcorn.

1. Jesus spoke of Hell as a literal place, describing it in graphic {scary} terms (Matt. 10:28;13:40-42; Mark 9:43-44).

2. Hell is as literal as Heaven (Psalm 11:4-6) and as eternal as Heaven (Matthew 25:46). {You can't believe in Heaven and not also believe in Hell.}

3. Hell is a place of punishment (Matthew 25:41; Rev. 20:10).

4. Hell will also be inhabited by people who do not accept God's gift of the Savior (Revelation 20:12-15).

5. Hell is a horrible place of suffering and everlasting destruction (Matthew 13:41,42; 2 Thessalonians 1:9).

6. In Hell people are conscious, regret-filled, retaining all their capacities and desires with no hope for any fulfillment for all eternity (Luke 16:22-31).

Let me also add that people don't just hang out together. Isolation is a key factor in Hell.

Trust me, you do not want to go there. And there will be no beer.

Twenty Four

Choices - Part Three of Three

James 4:7-8a
Submit yourself, then, to God. Resist the devil and he will flee from you. Come near to God and he will come near to you.

I have quoted another version of the second part of that verse in one of my talks for years…draw near to God and he will draw near to you. I have used this verse to encourage women to take the step to spend time alone with God, and he will answer when you call…he promises to be found by those who seek him.

But it was just this morning when reading the entire verse again that I saw the opposite promise that's at play here.

Resist the devil = he'll go away.

Come near to God = he'll come to you.

And I would bet that the counterpoints of each of these are true as well.

Come near to the devil = he'll willingly join you in your life's activities. (And I do not mean that you have to set out to become a devil worshipper for this to be the case. Every person is serving one of these two powers with their life choices. You must consciously choose to follow after God, otherwise, by default, you are following the enemy…even if you don't think that you are.)

Resist God = he'll leave you alone. He will grant your request. He gave us the gift of free will. He doesn't want robots, he wants relationship. If you want him in your life, he'll be so pleased, but if you don't, he'll let you live your own life, and will continue to grant that request into eternity.

Which one are you choosing?

Twenty Five

Going After the Heart

I consider myself a good parent. Not a great parent, but a good one. I feel self-taught in a lot of ways as my chosen path changed drastically when I decided to follow Jesus at the age of fifteen, not being raised in a Christian home. So things that maybe I would've been okay with if Christ weren't a major part of my life just aren't okay.

Just yesterday I had to tackle two tough issues with my kids, one each. One had to do with disobedience and respect, the other on cheating and integrity. Now, I think I know how I would've handled each as a "good parent", even a couple weeks ago. Usually with a consequence and some explanation of sorts as to why what they did was wrong.

But I am going through a great parenting book in my new small group, and it's making me see the bigger picture of why my children are really under my care. It's reminding me that my main job is to prepare them for adulthood, being on their own, making wise, godly decisions on their own…and it occurred to me that I only have six and seven years left with them to do this.

So I'm going after their hearts, because I don't just want to temporarily change a behavior, I want to change how they think and feel about themselves and others and God. I'm letting the sting of their choices last a little longer this week. My typical explanation was a bit deeper, a bit quieter (meaning, I didn't try to impart wisdom through yelling at them), and I made sure they both knew that the reason I wasn't letting these things just go is because I love them too much to do that. It's the harder approach, the slower approach, the approach that requires more wisdom, creativity and patience on my part. But I'm counting on the fact that it will be worth it in the long run.

So I'm going after their hearts, and I'm praying Jesus does too.

Twenty Six

Live and Let Live

My son, for whatever reason, cannot stand when his sister does something wrong. Or something that's not even actually wrong but that just bothers him. A lot of his sentences start like this, "Mom, Sara just…"

I've been working on this with him. Usually, my response is something like, "Baby, how does this affect your life in any way?" Because, truthfully, it's not like he's telling on her for hitting him in the head with a baseball bat or something. It's things like her accidentally leaving the bathroom light on. Or choosing to buy her own lunch. Really. Totally non-Jack-related things.

Last year, this conversation took place before school. Setting: I was in the kitchen, Sara was by the front door, Jack was in his bedroom. I yelled to Sara, "Are you bringing your lunch or buying your lunch?" Sara, "Buying." Jack, "Waste of money, Sara." Sara, "Live and let live, Jack."

I love it. Live and let live. No, this isn't a knock-off of the James Bond flick, "Live and Let Die", though sometimes I'm sure that phrase could fit into our family situations just as nicely.

Nope, it's a quote I've picked up over the past year that has revolutionized my life to such an extent, I wanted to get it into my children's heads and hearts.

Basically, it means, focus on your own life…not in a self-centered way, but in a 'my hands are full enough just trying to live a God-glorifying life…so full I can't be bothered being all judgy and critical of anyone else' way.

And let live. Well, that just means to let others live their own lives. Stop controlling. Stop butting in. Stop judging. Stop criticizing. Stop giving your two cents unless asked, and even then, think twice. You can still pray for, but stop being the Holy Spirit, or the mother (unless, of course, you are the mother).

Just plain you go live your life and I'll go live my life and things will be much more peaceful. (I'm telling you, it works.)

Sara has taken to this much more quickly than Jack. She seems to have no problem letting others live their own lives. She is not one to tattle. She just takes care of her own stuff.

Jack, on the other hand, almost can't help himself. He's the self-appointed cop of his sister, with an invisible notepad in hand jotting down all her missteps. Poor things. (Him and Sara.) That's no way to live.

One night, he was so upset over three things that Sara had done that bugged him. He wasn't upset about anything in his own life, just stuff Sara had done. So, I gave him my little pep talk and I prayed for him, asking Jesus to help Jack, just for that one night, to let go of at least one of those things. I don't know if it worked.

But yesterday, we had a breakthrough. Sara was in her bedroom working on homework, radio on. Jack was in the dining room also doing homework. I went to Sara's door and asked her to turn it down, even suggesting that she might be able to concentrate better with it off (she, shockingly, disagreed), but I didn't press it because it had been a suggestion. She turned it down though and I walked back out.

Apparently, she didn't do something to Jack's liking, because he said, "Mom, Sara…" Then he stopped himself. He sighed.

"What, hon?" I asked.

"Sara…", he said. Another sigh. "Never mind," he said, "I'm just going to live and let live on this one."

I walked over, told him I was proud of him, and kissed him on the head. I'll take that as progress.

Twenty Seven

Sideways

I really do believe that every person walking around on this planet is carrying within himself or herself some pain or disappointment or sadness. And I'm willing to, again, be so bold as to say that if you claim that you're not, you're lying. Or completely unaware.

And I really do believe that there are two camps of people in this world. Those who acknowledge their pain and those who don't, for a multitude of reasons.

For those of us who do acknowledge its existence, there are two choices. Ignore it. Or deal with it. And if you're fortunate enough to have Jesus in your life, he is hands down the best companion through pain.

But for those of us who don't acknowledge it, who honestly cannot see or feel their pain or, maybe worse yet, who see it and feel it but don't know what to do with it, one thing typically happens, though it may show itself in many forms. It comes out sideways. Love that image. Meaning, it comes out in anger at someone else or mistreatment of yourself or an addiction to alcohol or food or shopping or any manner of things.

The pain will come out, because it has to, it just won't come out appropriately.

It's these people that I understand, because I used to be one, I'm just realizing. I was a very sad woman fifteen some years ago. But my sadness didn't come out. Anger came out in its place, and it wasn't pretty. Along with talking too much to too many people. And perhaps, a small shopping addiction, if truth be told.

I'm grateful to say that I'm just not that sad anymore, which means I don't yell as much, nor do I talk to as many people about inappropriate things, nor do I shop. Well, okay, recovery is a process.

But because I've been there – in the role of "what's really going on deep inside that's making me act like this" – I cannot only understand, but I can remember the loneliness that goes with the covering up. And I feel compassion for this sector of people who live sideways. It's a sad way to live, it's an unexamined way to live, it is a hard-to-truly-connect-with-God-and-others way to live. And I don't wish it on anyone.

So, if you think you might be hurting, or pushing down some kind of hurt, take a deep breath or two, say a prayer, get some help, and start dealing with the thing. It will be difficult, I guarantee it. But the view from this side of the pain is outstanding.

Twenty Eight

Kicked the Devil in the Teeth

I was doing some ironing yesterday, getting ready to head out of town for a speaking gig, and this is what I heard running through my head, "Who do you think you are going and giving a talk on relationships?"

See, I had just had a little thing with someone the evening before and though we worked it out the best we could, my enemy (satan, the devil, the father of lies, whatever you want to call him) likes to push my buttons when it comes to my speaking and my perception of my competency. Well, maybe not even my competency in actually being able to speak in public, but my ability to have anything of value to say when my relationships sometimes go through ups and downs, as well as the whole hypocrite thing that I have a hard time shaking. *You just messed up last night and you're going to go tell women how to resolve conflict? Hypocrite...* You know, stuff like that.

But here's the thing about following Jesus for a while...you start to see through the enemy's tricks. Because he doesn't have a ton of them. He sort of recycles his ploys over and over again. So, this is what I did. I spoke, outloud, things like, *Who do I think I am to go give a talk about relationships? I think I'm a child of God who's doing the best she can. I think I've been given a spirit of power and of love and of a sound mind, and not a spirit of fear. I think I have the mind of Christ. I think I can do all things through Christ who strengthens me. And by the way, I don't walk up there and tell them that I've got my act together. I'm about as authentic and vulnerable as I can get. So, back off!*

Then I sat down at my computer and emailed a few close friends for prayer. I got some great eyes-on-Jesus kind of encouragement from my girls and I kept walking.

Fast forward to this morning. I am giving my talk and it's feeling kind of blah. It's the same talk that I gave two days prior and I had then felt great about it. But this time, no real reason in particular, blah. And then I sat at my book table with maybe a small handful of gals coming up to chat. So I'm thinking to myself, okay, well, if the only thing that came out of this was getting to catch up with two old friends, that was good enough for me.

But that wasn't good enough for Jesus. Nope. Jesus had something else in mind.

Because a gal walked up to my table, pulled a stool beside me, sat down, and started to simultaneously cry and tell me her story. I thought it would be a relationship-y thing, but it wasn't. I pulled her into the next room for some privacy and she tells me that she's had a hole inside since she was a little girl. That she's been searching for years for something that's missing but she doesn't know what it is.

And so right then and there I had the privilege of telling her my story of meeting Jesus for the first time, and told her, genuinely, that he is my closest friend. That life is still, I believe I said, "freaking hard", but that he comes in and gently begins to rearrange things. To heal things. To fill up that hole. And then we prayed together and she started a relationship of her own with Jesus.

It was beautiful. I was in awe of being able to be used like that. And then as I drove back home to Illinois, I remembered the battle with the enemy just the afternoon before, and I realized that I had just kicked the devil in the teeth...take that, I thought.

And then I thought, doesn't he realize that when he attacks, he just makes me stronger? *Sucker.*

Twenty Nine

Take Another Little Piece of My Heart

My feelings were hurt today. I shared something with someone that was pretty intimate, fairly vulnerable. Something, frankly, that I didn't want to share. And it wasn't received well. My heart was not handled gently. Which stinks, because I hate when it's not. And because, I really am trying to work on handling other people's hearts more gently.

So I turned on some music and let Jesus put me back together again. I am unlike Humpty Dumpty in that way. I can be put back together. In fact, sometimes in just minutes. I went into my bathroom to cry and came out maybe a half hour later, with a full heart, worshiping, encouraged, strengthened for the task ahead of me.

You see, I imagined giving the pieces of my heart to Jesus and I felt him tell me that not only would he gladly put them back together the right way, he would somehow put them back in a different shape, in a more beautiful way. Each and every time it's broken. Each and every time I bring it to him for mending.

And he does. I've had my heart smashed open over the years, cracked open, run over, split in two, split in to a thousand. And each time I bring it back to Jesus, he takes my tears and my words, both audible and not so much, and my worship, and my request for help and healing and filling, and he gently remedies, renews, renovates that broken thing, and hands it back to me more than all better.

It doesn't always happen in minutes…sometimes it's taken years, but he does it. And I think I'm finding that not only does he delight in me coming to him with my broken heart in my hands, but somehow, it's stronger, even if just a bit, each time he has to spend extra time with it.

Thirty

No Fear

I John 4:18
There is no fear in love. But perfect love drives out fear, because fear has to do with punishment. The one who fears is not made perfect in love.

I don't understand this verse. What does fear have to do with love?

I do not consider myself a fearful person. I used to be, perhaps. Quite the worrier. But then I started doing things, like, you know, public speaking and going to third world countries that were dangerous and stuff, and now I know that I can really do anything through Christ.

Okay, but here's the thing. I have a couple mini-phobias:

I'm not a fan of glass elevators.

Or escalators.

Or heights in general.

Or coming home to a dark, empty house.

Or sleeping in my own home when no one else is there.

Or driving on two-lane roads. (By the way, this one started because an old friend was telling me that it was much more dangerous, actually, to drive on two-lane roads than interstates. That was his effort at putting a stop to my then interstate-driving fear. It worked. But only by transference, I'm afraid.) Specifically at night. More specifically those that are 55 miles an hour. Most specifically Route 47, which is right by my house, so I need it to get to about fifty percent of my life.

I think that's it. I maybe don't like snakes, but I rarely see those, so not worth mentioning on the list.

Now, I know that this may sound immature. In fact, when I told someone about the two-lane highway new fear of mine (which, by the way, can be justified by what seems to be an inordinate number of accidents within ten minutes of my house lately), the response that I got was, judgmentally, "What's there to be afraid of on Route 47?" *Never mind*, I said. But here's the thing. Though I have mini-phobias, I still make myself go in glass elevators and up high and on escalators and sleep in my house alone and walk into a dark, empty house, and drive on 47.

Because I have a bigger fear. That if, just once, I accommodate any of those mini fears, I will accommodate it the next time, and the next time. And then I won't, you know, go up and down in public. And I won't come home at night. And I won't drive to fifty percent of my life anymore. So I don't accommodate. I just do the thing. The yucky, scary, I feel like a five-year-old thing. In fact, this Friday, I get the wonderful opportunity to do several of these all in one night. Yippee. I almost cancelled because I was scared, but that judgmentally snotty retort about 47 made me decide to face my fears.

And so maybe this is, in part, what this verse means. I know I am loved. With an over-the-top kind of love. And though I've been around long enough to know that just because my Creator loves me does not mean he will not allow bad things to happen to me, I know that I'm held through whatever might happen. And so, maybe because I'm loved and know it to my core, and know that I'll be held come what may, I can do those yucky, scary things. I can maybe even still be a little scared doing them, just as long as it doesn't stop me. Because then fear would win out, which means love would not. And I'm not okay with that.

So, hand me the car keys, point me to the nearest escalator, and you just watch me walk into the fear, and not away from it.

Thirty One

Sorry...Again

I messed up today. Messed up is too much of a kid glove phrase. It also sounds accidental. Or like I spilled something.

So I'll rephrase for accuracy and authenticity. I sinned today. It was something that I hadn't done in awhile, something that I've been working on.

So needless to say, I was angry with myself. So disappointed. And, because of the current level of intimacy with Jesus, felt so immediately disconnected.

I hate sinning. At first, I did what I usually do when I sin. That is, when I actually acknowledge it to myself. I told Jesus I was sorry. I went to my Bible and read Psalm 51, reminding myself that it was God I had just sinned against. And then I turned to I John 1:9 that says, "If you confess your sin, God is faithful and just and will forgive you of your sin and cleanse you from all unrighteousness." Which was good to hear, because I immediately wanted reconnection. I wanted to get back in his good graces as soon as I could.

So I told him I was sorry. Then, outloud, I claimed the promise that I was forgiven and clean and restored and could move on. Because I didn't feel like it. In fact, hours later, I'm still under a dark cloud that I might not shake until the morning. But that's actually my problem. Because it's not like the forgiveness will kick in with tomorrow's new mercies and I have to wait until then for the results. It kicked in the moment I asked for it.

Which leads me to a new reason why I hate sin. Because it makes me very self-aware. Too self-focused. Hard times do this to me, making me look down and in. Accomplishments do this to me, making me look around yet somehow still in. And sin does this to me, making me hang my head, shaming myself, making faces at myself in the proverbial mirror, not wanting to believe Truth.

And I was reminded of the Jesus of a couple days ago, who is the same today and yesterday and tomorrow, who was casually leaning against my door jam chewing gum (in my head, people…don't leave a ton of comments), and the thing I felt him say to me then, "Eyes on Me, baby," is the same thing I felt him say to me again. As in, *it's over. You said you were sorry. I forgave you. It might happen again. But we'll deal with it then.* Snapping to get my attention, *eyes back on Me.*

He is so good to me. So gentle. He loves me so much. He restores me. And if only I remember this, it just might stop me from doing the stupid thing again.

Thirty Two

Roll Some Stones Away

Right after I made the decision to follow Christ when I was fifteen years old, a sweet family took me under their wings. I spent a lot of time with my youth pastor, his wife and their four beautiful children. I'd go over to hang out, to attempt to learn to cook (some things just can't be learned by some people), to watch their kids. But it was more than that. So much more than that. My youth pastor's wife listened to me. As if, and I know this is such a cliché, but as if I were the only person in the world and she couldn't wait to hear what was in my head and heart. She listened to my dreams. She asked to listen to my poetry. We kept a journal together when I went away to college. She showed me how to be a follower of Christ, how to be a wife, how to be a mom, how to be a friend. She made me want to be some of these things (wife and mom) when I hadn't wanted to before. I don't know where I'd be, frankly, if she hadn't poured and poured and poured into me.

A few years after I got married and started to attend a church with my husband, I met a woman who had been married a while longer than I had been. Who was farther along in her faith. Who had walked with Christ through a hard marriage season of her own. And, if I recall, she approached me to get together and talk about marriage for awhile. She also listened. She shared her life and her struggles and how Christ got her through some things. She challenged me. She prayed for me and with me. I recall one time, sharing something so intimate with her, and watching tears roll down her cheeks, and she gripped my hand and held it for awhile and said she had no idea. I don't know where I'd be, frankly, if she hadn't poured and poured and poured into me.

I now have a woman in my life who I've known for several years but who I turned to in a dark time recently. Oh, sweet Charlotte. Everyone should have a Charlotte in their lives. She has listened. In fact, she has heard *it all*. The whole story. The whole horrible story with all the details that no one but Jesus had known up til that point. She has shown grace. She has prayed. She has given the best advice, over and over and over again, that I have ever gotten in my entire life. She has held me up. She has looked me in the eyes and told me it was hard but that I could do it. That I could keep walking. But that, and I know what she meant when she said this, if I ever chose to stop walking, there would be grace there too.

Author Jane Rubietta writes, "We need someone to help move the stones. Jesus didn't move the stone himself, and neither did Lazarus {when called out of his own tomb, three days dead}. Instead, Jesus appointed someone else to do the work that could be done with human hands. Who will help move your stones? This is no task for a dead woman. This is a task for a friend, a friend not afraid of stench, not afraid of decay, not worried about the deterioration of soul and spirit and body that comes from living in this world." She goes on to say, "That's a friend. If you must be dead in a cave, make sure you have a friend posted at the stone of your heart to roll it away at the right time."

Charlotte rolled away my stone at the most dead point of my life, she being able to because she had been dead and was now fully alive herself. And then she told me to roll all the worries and hurt onto Jesus, that he could handle it. I don't know where I'd be, frankly, if she hadn't poured and poured and poured into me.

And now it's my turn. I've never been more ready, or more afraid, to help others become free. To roll some stones away of friends in need. I look back at these three women who poured and poured, and I thank each one, and I thank Jesus for such gifts, and I walk on, taking the hands of two women who need me. May I continue the legacy, live up to what Jesus is calling me to do, be just half of the gentleness and the wisdom and the joy that these women were to me.

Thirty Three

Kingdom Coming

I almost wrote this for my Facebook status: "Just built the Kingdom a little bit more this morning," as a follow-up to what I posted earlier: "This morning holds three women spending time with Jesus. Only Good can come."

And though I feel that's true – that the Kingdom was built in that kitchen with the three of us, and three of their children at our feet – that belies something that I don't believe to hold true. And that is that Kingdom work is only spiritual stuff.

Because my Facebook status could say what I wanted it to say but it would not just be because I met with two women and we opened the Word and asked Jesus to change us.

I have built the Kingdom a little bit more this morning because I woke up at 5:25am so I could make breakfast for my kids.

And because I prayed with them before they walked out the door to catch the bus.

And because I spent time with Jesus getting filled up.

And because I held my tongue with my husband.

And because I prayed in the car on the way to my friend's house.

And because I gave the girls' hugs and we prayed and we read the Word and we talked and I reached over to touch an arm when tears came and we prayed some more, for healing, for Light to shine into us, for the enemy to back off.

And because I thanked Jesus once I got back in my car for letting me be a part of this, for being his partner in helping some women hopefully move a bit farther ahead with him.

And because on my way home I stopped to take a walk along a path and took in deep breaths and praised Jesus for his creation and let the colors and the cool breeze stir my soul.

And because I made myself some hot chocolate and finished a good book, and thanked him for both good things.

And because when my son called from school just now asking if I could bring him an allergy pill, I did it without making him feel like he just put me out.

And because after giving him his pill, I put my hand on his shoulder and prayed for him in the middle of the school hallway, and he let me and told me he loved me.

And because I'm writing these words right now.

And because I will go on to have a little lunch and to welcome my kids home from their day and to make my family dinner and to help with homework (this will only be Kingdom building if I don't mutter thirty-seven times how much I hate doing homework though).

And because I have been talking to Jesus throughout and plan to continue to do so. Because, as Jane Rubietta writes, "Just a smile, and we hasten the kingdom." Because it's all these things and so much more and so much less that help us pull heaven down here and all around us.

Because I need a little more of the Kingdom in my daily life. Because my heart's desire is "Thy Kingdom come, Thy will be done, on earth as it is in heaven."

Thirty Four

Running on Empty

Whenever I start something new that I'm not sure I can do, or whenever I take on a task that I know God has called me to, I hear voices. Not like "prepare to be taken to the moon in a spaceship" kind of voices, though that might be kinda cool.

But things like "you don't know enough about AIDS to lead that team" and "who do you think you are to give a talk on relationships" and "seriously, you're going to lead these women? you can't lead yourself… hell-o, remember yesterday?"

Nice.

Today, I took on a new task. But yesterday had to happen first. Yesterday was a day of being beaten down. Of a few things inside breaking and then shifting. Of being reminded, as if I didn't already know this, that I have not by any means arrived, thereby ensuring my humility. Of being depleted of words and of what to do next. Of feeling like I hadn't really changed all that much like I thought I had.

So I woke up this morning doubting some things. And totally empty. Empty of, well, myself. Which I realized, as it turns out, is a really great way to come to God and a really great place to be before starting something new.

Because this pretty much guaranteed that I wouldn't be showing up to this new thing with all my answers, in all my energy, with all my strength. Because my answers didn't quite cut it yesterday, and my energy was long gone, and my strength…well, what strength?

And when you're empty, you are more apt to go looking to be filled. Thankfully, I came to the Source of Life for my filling today. I don't always, I'm sorry to say, but this morning I did.

And the Spirit led me to these words from Psalm 63:

⁷ Because you are my help,
*   I sing in the shadow of your wings.*
⁸ My soul clings to you;
*   your right hand upholds me.*

And I pictured myself sitting closely, as closely as I could get, under the wings of the Most High. I can sit there because he is my help and my fortress and I trust him. And I pictured my soul clinging to him. And I pictured him just to my left as his right hand held me up and held me close. And I asked him to fill me with his energy, with his joy, with his gentleness, with his love. That his Holy Spirit would fill up all of my empty places, and today, there were many.

I walked away not as thirsty, not so empty, not as weary, not so defeated. I walked away ready. Am I competent in my own strength to be what these two friends need, to roll away some stones? No. But II Corinthians 12:9a says, *"But he said to me, 'For my grace is sufficient for you, for my power is made perfect in {your} weakness.'"*

Not perfect for these girls…don't need to be. They're not looking for it or expecting it or need it. Just doing the best I can…as filled up as I can be.

Thirty Five

Sometimes It's Hard to be the Mom

I just sent an unwilling child to school. Not a sick child, but a sad one. You need to know that I am not without empathy in this area. I used to be the unwilling child.

My entire seventh grade year was my unwilling year. First year of junior high. At a new school. Didn't know a soul. New home. Two less people in my family. I played the guilt card. The scared card. The sick card. The sad card. *A lot.*

I was going to say that I don't know how my mom handled it…and when I say 'it', I mean me. But I do know. She let me stay home…often. Then, I was thrilled. Looking back, I know I can't make the same decision for my son. Because it fed into my fears and my sadnesses.

My son is adjusting to middle school. It's been bumpy. It's been more homework than he's ever had and friendship politics that make me want to go right over there and knock some kid-heads together and changing classes and being on the small side and his football team's losing streak and everybody else buys hot lunch so dot dot dot. You remember all of this, right? I sure do.

I remember the dread. It would start the night before. It was worse on Sunday nights after two nice days of being home with my mom.

Jack's dread started last night in the car on the way home from a great afternoon of playing with his cousins. We got in the car and, bam, sadness, quietness. He didn't tell me until two hours later when he was getting ready for bed that that's what the sadness was about. *I don't feel like I want to go to school tomorrow*, he said. *Oh*, I said softly, and held him.

This is so hard. My kid is not trying to get out of anything. He's the kind of kid who was mad at himself for getting sick last year and ruining his perfect attendance record. So for him to not want to go, well, that says something.

But I told him that I wouldn't be doing him any favors by letting him stay home because of fear or sadness. Just like I needed to make myself drive on 47, he needs to make himself go to school. And I need to help him make himself. Even if I can tell he's about to cry. Even if I cry.

So we prayed. We prayed last night and we prayed this morning, twice. I will pray throughout the day. I'm praying for things like bravery and strength. I'm reminding him that he can do all things through Christ. That Jesus is right there with him. Things like that. But my loudest and most repeated request is this...*Jesus, be real to my son. Be his best friend. Show up for him in this. This would be a great time to show Jack who you really are.* I hope he does. I obviously believe he can otherwise I wouldn't keep praying.

My mom let me stay home during seventh grade because she loved me. I'm making my son go to sixth grade for the same reason.

Thirty Six

Radical

A friend just sent me a text encouraging me to be radical for Jesus today. I had three simultaneous thoughts.

What a great friend.

What a great text.

How do I be radical for Jesus if I'm going to be at home all day?

Really. I get how to if I'm, for instance, running an AIDS Team meeting, or preparing to fly off to a third world country, or speaking at a women's event, or meeting with someone to talk through how we can allow Scripture to transform our lives. But how do I live radically for Jesus when I'm doing laundry and marinating salmon?

I can eat fewer cookies. Seriously.

I can watch less television.

I can go for a run or walk or do some kind of exercise that shows God I actually do appreciate this healthy body he's given me.

I can pray a bit longer than usual…for my children, my friends, my world.

I can read something about HIV that will build up my knowledge and therefore my passion.

I can write something for my next book that will move it one day forward.

I can look again at those few verses that for some reason I couldn't seem to memorize and take another crack at them.

I can do some investigating about my next trip or two.

I can speak the truth to myself. Days alone at home can be long and quiet…which I happen to treasure…but I tend to, sometimes perhaps, talk to myself a bit. And sometimes what I say is not only unkind (*idiot, why did you spill that?*) but untrue (*she hasn't responded because she doesn't like you…*). So I can start saying true things to myself when I'm alone and in the quiet.

I can choose to not waste my day, and therefore my life.

It's all about redefining radical. Radical doesn't have to mean being burned at the stake or standing on a street corner proclaiming the world's end. It can mean looking at the life of Jesus and getting to know him well enough as a person, and loving him enough, to know what he would want me to be and do.

I better get busy.

Thirty Seven

Radical Check-Up

So, I thought I would look back on my today and see how I did in the radical department...if I took any of my own advice. Thought it also might enhance my credibility a bit if you see that I occasionally actually do live my life the way I write.

So, here was my list:

I can eat fewer cookies.

I really did eat fewer cookies. In fact, at one point, I went for one but instead grabbed an apple.

I can watch less television.

Finished reading my small group chapter instead of plopping down for ten minutes of channel surfing.

I can go for a run or walk or do some kind of exercise that shows God I actually do appreciate this healthy body he's given me.

Yep, even though the actual running part sucked for some reason (just one of those days). The cool-down walk ended up being an intimate time with Jesus, though, as did the impromptu long way home only to find myself gasping and giggling at the colors of the trees around each bend, and waving my hands (okay, hand) out of my sunroof out of sheer joy at the beauty of this day.

I can pray a bit longer than usual...for my children, my friends, my world.

Wrote out some prayers for my family and friends. Things I maybe wouldn't have prayed about if I hadn't just written the original blog moments before.

I can read something about HIV that will build up my knowledge and therefore my passion.

Read a 39-page thesis that reminded me why I care so much about this issue.

I can write something for my next book that will move it one day forward.

Truth be told, I spent only about five minutes on this today. But there's always tomorrow.

I can look again at those few verses that for some reason I couldn't seem to memorize and take another crack at them.

Well, I did a refresher course on my first batch of memorized ones, and I re-read those stubborn final six that are tripping me up.

I can do some investigating about my next trip or two.

Yep, sent some emails and looked into flights. Prayed about them again too.

I can speak the truth to myself. Days alone at home can be long and quiet...which I happen to treasure...but I tend to, sometimes perhaps, talk to myself a bit. And sometimes what I say is not only unkind (*idiot, why did you spill that?*) but untrue (*she hasn't responded because she doesn't like you...*). So I can start saying true things to myself when I'm alone and in the quiet.

Didn't spill anything today. :)

I also did do the laundry, per usual, but I prayed for each person in my family as I sorted. And I did marinate some salmon but I thanked God that we have enough food. And I did eat a cookie or two, because life is for the enjoying.

I can choose to not waste my day, and therefore my life.

Hopefully, I didn't.

A little self-evaluation now and then is good for the soul.

And Sheli, thank you for a better, more intentional, day than I would've had without your text of encouragement.

Thirty Eight

Talk to Me

So I'm walking outside and I ask Jesus to talk to me. *I've been doing all the talking lately,* I say. *Talk to me. Tell me something I don't know.*

Here's what my heart heard:

I love you, sweet girl.

I love you if you go for a run, if you walk instead, or even if you sit on the couch.

I love you if you memorize another twenty-seven verses or if you never memorize another one the rest of your life.

I love you if you run that 5k you're thinking about next year or if you just think about running that 5k.

I love you if you go on all three trips next year or if you don't go on any.

I love you if you barely hang on with that thing or if it completely changes and you're able to flourish in it.

I love you if you write this book or if you never write another word.

I love you if everyone else likes you or if you feel that no one does.

I love you when you sin and when you refrain.

I love you when you yell and when you hold your tongue.

I love you when you eat an apple or when you eat five cookies.

I love you on your accomplishing days or on your shopping days.

I love you if you do everything or if you do nothing.

Lay it all down. Give it all to me. I've got it. I've got you.

I love you.

I needed that.

Thirty Nine

Good King

Today's text (not as in Scripture, but as in what popped up on my cell phone this morning compliments of my encouragement fairy): *The King is calling your name.*

Sweet, sweet words to my soul. I sat down on the couch with my tea, under a blanket, a candle lit, my Bible and journal next to me. I closed my eyes and pictured a King, my King, calling my name…I pictured him looking for me, waiting for me. Beth Moore says God can't wait for us to wake up each morning. He's like a parent of a newborn who can't get enough, who has to tiptoe into the nursery during naptime for one more look. He loves us just that much.

And he's not waiting for me so he can shame me, to give me marching orders (though sometimes I do ask for them), to point out how long it's been since I've entered His holy presence. He takes delight in me as a Father with a treasured daughter. He wants to know how I'm doing (even though he already knows). He wants to know what's hurting me (he knows that too). According to Song of Solomon, he loves the sound of my voice and he thinks my face is lovely. He thinks I'm precious in his sight. He calls me the apple of his eye. He takes great delight in me, he quiets me with his love, and he, as King on the throne, sings a song over me. He knows me by name.

Revelation 2:17b says, "To {her} who overcomes, I will give {her} a white stone with a new name written on it, known only to {her} who receives it."

So, he knows my actual right-now name, but I think, when he's calling me into his presence, when he's singing that song over me, I imagine it with my new name falling from his lips, and flowing in the lyrics. My new name that I don't know yet. My new name that only a King can give me.

I'm overwhelmed yet again by this great love. It's a big love. It's not always a safe love, according to C.S. Lewis, but it's a good love. It holds me up. It pulls me through. It carries me through a day. It's carried me through my life.

"Be at rest once more, O my soul, for the LORD *has been good to you."* Psalm 116:7

So, so good. As only a King can be.

Forty

Not Alone

What I've got today is an overwhelming gratitude for my friends. A deep gratitude. An I'm-just-realizing-how-God-has-used-them-to-fill-in-the-gaps kind of gratitude. This isn't just me thinking it's cool that I get to go out to eat with them, light and fluffy, kind of thing.

No, it's much deeper than that.

Just this week alone, I've had fireside discussions with two.

I've had breakfast and conversation with one.

I've had encouraging texts and a voicemail from another.

I've gotten celebratory words of affirmation via email from another.

I've gotten sounding-board advice from another.

I've shared dinner and joy with another.

I think I might've teared up with each one as well. But in a good way.

I've also had morning candlelit tea every day this week with another special Someone.

My life is full relationally. My soul is well tended. My thoughts are fully heard. My burdens are carried. My joys are shared. My heart is at capacity.

And just when I think it's not...when it's emptied out by something that life or my enemy, or a combination, puts in my path, it mysteriously gets filled right back up again.

I don't walk alone. I never have. And I never will.

Like I said, *overwhelming.*

Forty One

Warmth or the Wind?

I was reflecting on some significant advice I'd been given in the past couple years. Advice might not be the right word. Someone else's opinion maybe. I was given this same opinion twice, within months, but one was cloaked in harshness, the other in gentleness, and looking back, I'm amazed at the difference in how I took it, and in how it took root in me.

This is what I was told first, and it was written in caps, which connotes yelling in my mind, "I'M NOT SAYING IT'S YOUR FAULT BUT YOU DO HAVE A PART IN IT!" O-kay. You know how my mind heard that? *It is your fault and you're really the only one who's contributed to it and therefore the only one who needs to work on it.* But maybe that's just oversensitive me.

I balked at that opinion. I yelled. I cried. I begged God to make the thing not be my fault. I shrunk back. I recoiled like a turtle finding refuge in its shell. I shut down. I was…broken. Not broken-hearted, though I was. But broken. Something broke in me with those rough, punitive words. I had been blaming myself for years upon years already…yet I had been hoping someone would come along and quietly say, "It is not your fault." So when I heard those loud words, well, the accusation they carried resonated with what I'd been telling myself all along and it was almost too much for me to bear.

But then, I found a different source. I was accused of finding something that I wanted to hear. That may be true. I'm not above that. But I don't think that's what happened in this case. I sought out another opinion. I went to find out if the first set of words were true and what that would really mean then.

But the second set of words came differently. The second set was spoken more slowly. In tenderness. In whispers. In emotional lower case.

you did not cause this. you cannot control this. you cannot stop this. however, there are some things you can work on in you.

Oh, my heart thought. And my shoulders loosened, as did my jaw and my fists. If a soul could sigh, mine did deeply. I walked closer to the light, not away from it, because this light was kind and merciful, not blinding and unrelenting. And I sat in stillness for a little while, soaking up some healing. And then I set to work. Because there really were things I could work on. And I did.

But here's what's absolutely amazing to me, over a year later. Look back at the capitalized opinion. Then look at the lower-case one. They are, in essence, the very same message. But one made me cry and one made me change.

Which just reiterates a truth of the ages.

You can attract more flies with honey...

It will be the warmth of the sun that makes the man loosen his coat and leave it behind over the briskness of the wind every time...

Let your gentleness be evident to all...the Lord is near... Philippians 4:5

Oh, Lord, let me be that gentle voice in others' lives. Amen.

Forty Two

Thank You for Fallen Apples. Really.

I just finished reading a lovely book that stirred my soul. The thread that ran throughout was a commitment to being present in the moment you're in, being aware of the environment surrounding you.

I like to think that I'm attentive to details. I live a slower-paced life than the average person...a slower-paced life than I have ever lived before... and this is of my choosing. (It is also a gift from God.) So I have the time to stop and literally smell the roses if I like. I stop, from time to time, to take a walk on a path that wasn't on my to-do list. I'll sit with a cup of tea and no book in hand, sometimes outside, sometimes on my couch looking out the window.

But this book re-reminded me to stop more frequently, to linger a bit longer. To notice, to appreciate, to be grateful, to give thanks, to bless.

Yesterday, I watched my son in his room play with some cars. It was maybe two minutes, and he didn't know he was being watched, but I just watched him, thanking God for giving him to me. I noticed the hues in the sky as the clouds drifted along while the sun was setting. I gasped, actually gasped, at the tree tops as they were brushed with sunlight for perhaps half a minute. I wanted someone to stop and see it with me, but no one else was in the room. I saw the moon try to peak through. This was all from my spot on the couch.

I also sat with my pain last night. I did something to my neck a few days ago and it's been sore, giving me some trouble. Last night I acknowledged the pain to God and didn't, I don't think, ask him to take it away. Instead, I thanked him that it was a reminder of all the other nights that I go to bed with no discomfort at all and thanked him for a healthy body. I also thanked him for the reminder that I'm human and I have an end.

This morning when at a meeting, I listened when others spoke. Not just for what their words could do to help me fix my life or what I might say next if I were to take a turn, but just listened to validate their existence and their experience, and I thanked each person after they spoke.

And just a little while ago I was doing some yard work. (That sentence amuses me.) Even though I wasn't feeling well, I took on the task of putting fallen apples into a garbage can and bringing them to the compost pile. There were a lot of apples. It took me about an hour. It was not glamorous work. In fact, coupled with the soreness of my neck and a potential fever, I pretty much hated it. And I started off mumbling under my breath a bit. But then my son joined me and I didn't want to be a bad influence, so I started thanking Jesus out loud for things. Just a few things. I thanked him for the sun, for our beautiful yard, for apples... *not these apples*, I said, *because these are gross and this is a pain, but thank you for apples in general.* Jack smiled. When Jack went on to something else, I kept thanking Jesus for things. I thanked him for the fresh air and the ability to pick up an apple and toss it in a garbage can. Really, I did. Because that's no small thing.

Forty Three

Build the Bridge

I was talking with a friend who was telling me that she has been struggling with feeling a real disconnect with God. She's a fairly new believer and she says she's never really felt his presence. She got baptized, hoping that might kick it into high gear, but to no avail. (Let me rephrase...she got baptized out of obedience and was hoping that intimacy would ensue...she didn't do it *for* the closeness.) She's in a Bible study. She comes to church every Sunday. She serves. She prays. She has quiet times. And, nothin'.

Basically, I said, it sounds like you're having a very human spiritual experience.

I gave her some advice, because she was looking for advice. I suggested that she check her heart to make sure she wasn't in some kind of God-blocking sin. I suggested she commit to time with Jesus each day. I suggested she find a way she can serve that will be fulfilling. I suggested she speak truth out loud...tell herself things she knows...that she is saved, that the Holy Spirit does dwell inside of her, that she is loved completely. I suggested she realize that a lot of the spiritual walk is just doing the thing we know we should be doing and trusting that it's building a bridge between us and God.

And then I prayed that she would feel, tangibly feel, God's presence and peace. That he would speak to her in ways that she would notice. That her spiritual eyes would be open.

And the rest, really, is up to God.

Forty Four

Build the Bridge, Part Two

Here's what I also had wish I said to my friend.

I wish I told her to keep wanting more. That it is good to long for more of God. To not stuff the feelings down of wanting to feel him. To not chalk it up to "well, I guess that's all there is…"

Because there is so much more available. The abundant life *does* start now. Not when we break through eternity. Our eternal life, for those of us who know Christ, has begun. So has our abundant life.

I don't have the answers why some feel God as close as their breath day in and day out, and why some may live their entire Christian lives with only a glimpse.

But I know that I have seen both. I have walked through stretches of life where, other than nature itself, there is nothing that points to the truth of God in my life. And I have walked hand in hand with Jesus for sweet, sweet seasons.

So, my revised advice would be to pray for more awareness but also more desire. Because I would so much rather wish for something glorious that maybe only comes in slivers then give up on the glory altogether.

Forty Five

Exercise in Futility?

There are a lot of things that I do in life that, come to think of it, bring forth either zippo results or nothing like I had hoped.

Let's see. Anti-aging facial products. Though I know myself well enough to know that I will use them til my dying day, it has occurred to me that there is no way at all to know, really, if they work in the least.

Cooking. Yes, I do need to actually feed my family, but there are times that I spend way too much time, even for me, on something that turns out, let's just say, not so great. You know, where the kids prefer to go without dessert over having to finish the thing in front of them.

Television. I would bet that almost every moment I spend in front of the television is a colossal waste of time.

My son just did something that I fear was a complete waste of his time. We are the owners of a variety of outdoor cats. And just over the past couple days, a few of the kittens are declining. One has died. One has gone missing, along with her mother, and another is on its last breaths, we fear.

But Jack came home, saw the dying kitty and asked for permission to try to make it well again. Granted, in a heartbeat. He made the box-home that he created the night before a bit more comfortable. He brought out food and milk. Then he asked for a towel. And I watched my formerly-scared-to-pick-up-cats son reach down, pick up the dying kitten, and hold it gently in his arms for probably ten minutes, in the hopes of reviving it with his warmth and attention.

And I thought to myself, *that cat will probably be dead by the morning. There's an exercise in futility.*

But wait. Even if the cat dies, was that forty-five minutes of my son's life little more than just a waste of time? Did it do more than just put off our two-hour-long homework session?

I have a feeling it was bigger than that, no waste at all. Even if the cat doesn't make it.

I actually had a moment where I realized that my son was fighting back death because there is something in him that knows that death is not right. That kittens shouldn't die. That life is worth caring for, fighting for.

I do many things that are an actual waste of time.

I do many things that I think are important but aren't in the least.

I do many things that may feel like a waste of time, that may feel intangible perhaps if not a waste, but by no means are.

I pray. I write. I read. I hold hands. I send notes. I rub backs. I worship. I cry. I laugh. I hope. I long. I cling. And my son holds kittens that are dying hoping that they won't.

I call these exercises in great good, albeit sometimes invisible.

Forty Six

Remind Me

Went to spend time with a friend who is nursing a broken heart as we speak. It was two and a half hours of crying, talking, praying, walking, laughing and eating brownies and ice cream. *Hell-o*...that's how girls roll.

It was one of those really hard and yet simultaneously seamless things. I didn't want to do it. Not that I didn't want to spend time with her...I just didn't want to have to be spending time with her today because of what was going on with her. But today we did what friends do.

Now, I love the fun moments with my girlfriends. I love laughing until tears roll down my cheeks, laughing until I think I can't stand it anymore and I forget whatever hard thing is in my life at the moment.

But I love the hard times too. I love being a friend in a hard time. Not that I love having my friends go through hard things, but there's something that just plunges two people down deeper and closer when they have to hold on for dear life. When hands are intertwined and tears are coming and words are prayed...or sometimes sighs are prayed when there are no words...

I have good friends. Rephrase: I have been given simply amazing, life-changing, heart-taking-care-of, soul-tending, leaning-on-me while I-lean-on-them-right-back friends. I *love* them. And I love my life so much more because of them. Because of the emails. The texts. The Facebook comments. The inside jokes. The laughter.

Oh, but I love them so much more because I have cried in front of each one of them and I have held each one of their hands at some point and I have prayed with and been prayed for and I know that I know that I am loved for who I am by beautiful, precious women.

Today was a reminder that one of the points of this life is to be tangible reminders to each other of what matters in life. Friends matter. Life matters. Death matters. Grieving matters. Healing matters. Love matters. Jesus matters. That's what today was for me, and I hope it's what it was for my friend.

Forty Seven

More than One Can Take

This has been a week of loss around my life. Small deaths, big deaths. Figurative deaths, literal deaths.

A friend lost her baby in a miscarriage. So many tears…so much sadness. My sorrow had possibly eclipsed the previous joy.

We have four less cats than we had a week ago. Two dead, two missing. I'm not even a cat fan, but come on…four in one week? That's not even all that hard on me, to be honest, but it's hard on my kids, and because of that, by default, hard on me. My son even made the comment, "They'd still be alive if I had…" The weight of the loss…

A friend shared something with someone that she shouldn't have…a loss of full trust, a loss of innocence.

A hope I had for a potentially life-changing experience was dashed.

A dream to publish a book about a story that I had hoped would bring encouragement to hurting people with the promise of redemption had a door closed on it.

I was almost in two car accidents within three hours of each other, both of which could've ended horribly.

Death. Loss. I'm feeling the weight of it today.

During my time with Jesus this morning, I listed these things and then I asked for comfort. A verse came to my mind immediately from Matthew 5:4. In the well-known Beatitudes, Jesus says, "Blessed are those who mourn for they will be comforted."

It is a *promise* that when I mourn, when I am going through something difficult or grieving the loss of something precious, I will in fact be comforted.

Today I chose to comfort myself by reminding myself that God is faithful. That he provides. That he has gotten me through much worse. That he can bring good from each one of these things. That he is the God who sees, completely and intimately aware of the ache that each one of these things pricks into my heart. And there is an ache.

But these things also remind me that life is precious. That there is much to be celebrated *as is*. That the dark helps us see how light the light really is. That even in the ache, I can simultaneously be a grateful girl...a very grateful girl.

I was thinking that I could use a little light...a little lift...but maybe he wants me to be that light for someone else.

Praise be to the God and Father of our Lord Jesus Christ, the Father of compassion and the God of all comfort, who comforts us in all our troubles, so that we can comfort those in any trouble with the comfort we ourselves have received from God. II Corinthians 1:3-4

Forty Eight

Stop Loss

About five years ago, something bad happened to a dear friend of mine. It plunged me into an almost six month depression as I took the thing on almost as my own.

Last week, something bad happened to another dear friend of mine. It didn't plunge me. I was as sad as if it were me for about one full day, with some random crying in the days that followed, still.

To be fair, the two events were different in some important ways, but they held similarities…they were both "why, God?" kinds of things… they both happened to people I care deeply about…they both brought deep pain.

Another similarity – neither happened directly to me. But that didn't stop me the first time around from sinking deep.

I think that something has changed in me since the first incident five years ago. Since then, I have had two large life difficulties. One was the kind of all-of-the-sudden thing that pounced on my life and the other was a waking up to the realization of a difficult thing that had already been there but I had been in denial about. In other words, since the first thing, I've had my own hard times to process life and God and faith and trials and how those things all fit together.

Also, I think there's been…at least, I hope there's been…some growth on my part. I cannot carry the weight of the world on my shoulders and around with me all day every day. I wasn't created to. My own issues are all I am supposed to handle. And in fact, when I grieve alongside someone appropriately, I am able to be there more for the person who is hurting in a way that is needed and desired, than if I were all wrapped up in my junk each time someone I knew was hurting.

The amount of loss and hurt in life has increased as I've gotten older… or, at the very least, I'm much more attuned to it. But, gratefully, the way that it hits me each time…even my own, I'm thankful to say…doesn't take me out at the knees and down below the surface any more.

And that's something I don't mind losing.

Forty Nine

You and Me and Her and Us and Him

Today has been a full relational day, mixed in with my normal routine.

I started my morning with some time with Jesus.

I had a forty-five minute phone conversation with a sweet girl looking for some advice. I shared some of my thoughts and prayed with her.

I received a text from a friend saying she was missing me. I texted back the same.

I sent an email to a mentor asking how to forgive someone. She wrote back a wonderful, loving answer.

I received another text from a friend saying she was looking forward to our time tonight and praying for me.

I received a phone call from a friend who is hurting emotionally and physically and I prayed for her while she drove to the doctor.

I then emailed a friend asking her to also pray for that hurting friend.

Over email, a friend reminded me of her son's doctor's appointment, so I prayed for that.

Over Facebook, another friend mentioned some health issues, so I prayed for her.

I helped my son with homework for, thankfully and amazingly, only fifteen minutes. (Is it my birthday?)

One of my children lied to me and so we had to have one of those talks. And he/she wrote me and God an apology letter.

And now I get to spend some time trying to partner with Jesus to bring freedom to two sweet girls and myself.

(And I'm an introvert.)

Besides that, I did a load of laundry, a load of dishes, cleaned three bathrooms, cleaned the kitchen, vacuumed two floors of my home, took a quick nap, took a quick run, made dinner, and wrote a little bit.

And it's all intertwined. We're all, really, just trying to get through life, and on really good days, we're just helping each other do it. I pray for someone, someone prays for me. I give advice to someone, someone advises me. I hurt for someone, someone hurts for me.

And God is at the center of it all. Drawing us closer to each other and closer to him. Speaking through us, healing through each other. It's beautiful and interwoven and what life is all about.

Fifty

Coping, Processing and Consolations

Last week, I had two significant no's tossed into my lap. Yesterday, a friend told me she got a big no as well and she didn't know how to process it. It was over something that she had been thinking about and praying about for a few months, something she thought God might be in. And then a human being told her no, she couldn't do it.

Let me first say that I don't know too many people who brighten up when told no. In fact, most of us start bristling at that word around the age of two, and start bucking against it around that time as well.

But seeing as no is a part of life, there are three things that I tell myself when it happens that help me, sometimes just a little, to enfold it into my life and keep walking.

First, God can and does speak through and lead through other people. So, perhaps, even though it's hard to hear, someone's no just might be God's no.

Second, let's just say that person was wrong. You've been told no over something that God intended to be a yes. First of all, I firmly believe that my willingness to do whatever God wants in that situation will go a long way and secondly, if I'm being held back from a God thing by someone else, well, I'm about to get down on my knees so the sweeping arm of God's justice misses me and spiritually knocks the no-giver in the metaphorical noggin. Meaning, God will deal with this person if they kept me from doing a God thing and I don't think it'll be pretty.

And third, this was a deep heart revelation that came to me after a season of praying with my husband about internationally adopting. I was on board. On board doesn't fully describe it. I had been looking at waiting child lists, knew where I wanted us to adopt from, figured where the child would sleep, et cetera, et cetera. We spent some time talking and praying and he came back with a no. A no that broke my heart like no other no had ever done. And as I began the grieving process, God's spirit spoke to mine as plain as day, "If you think he is able to thwart My plan for your life, than you're giving him way too much credit and Me not enough." Whoa…I had so needed to hear that.

So when the no's come, and they will keep coming, I will remind myself that God is bigger than all of them put together, and I just need to keep a willing, clean, yielded heart before him and let him worry about the details.

Fifty One

Seasons

I wish you could see where I live. It's actually smack dab in the middle of geographically-boring Illinois but I have to pretty much take back roads wherever I go, which is something I've always longed for. I don't live out in the boonies by any stretch of the imagination, but it's enough of a jaunt to get anywhere that it gives me time to really take in the nature that's along the way. And just today, as I was taking in the fact that it's the day after Thanksgiving, that I have Christmas music playing constantly (quite unlike me), that my tree is up, that most of my shopping is done, that my family letter is written, and that it's that in between moment in time where it's pretty cold but I'm still in my fall coat but wishing for snow that isn't here yet, I started to think about seasons.

First, I'm hugely grateful that I live in a place that actually has seasons (someone please make me read this again in February). I absolutely love that everything has its time and place. That just when we're sick of gray days, snow comes. And just when we've had it up to here with the snow, maybe literally, the sun peaks out and leaves start to bud. And just when we can't stand any more rain, it's hotter than hot and we can walk around in tank tops and flip flops. And when the heat has worn us down, the leaves start to change into brilliant colors and the sky is the bluest blue you've ever seen. It's long enough to appreciate, then gone long enough to miss it and want it again by the time it rolls back around.

And how much like life is that?

Right now I'm in a sweet season. It's quiet and slow paced. It's full of things I love…writing, speaking, reading, friends, days at a time in my jammies, sitting on my couch with a cup of tea soaking in my view that seems to change each day in some small nuance.

But I know that there are other seasons. Seasons of intense ministry, like when I am in the middle of preparing for some international travel, which I know is just around the bend.

Seasons of total blahs when I feel like I'm in a funk emotionally and spiritually despite doing all the things I normally do, sometimes despite trying even harder to connect.

Seasons of deep pain, sometimes brought on by my own choices, sometimes brought on by the thoughtless choices of others.

And seasons where all of this is mixed up together.

They all come and go. Just when we think we're bored with life, something comes that shifts the whole thing on its side. Just when we can't believe how blessed we are, well, sometimes a crisis rears its ugly head and the blessings are magnified in comparison. And sometimes when we just can't imagine walking through that hard thing for one more moment, light breaks through in splinters and it reminds us that we're not alone, that this thing of ours won't last forever, that we can get through it because we've gotten through worse just a season or two before.

Seasons. They come and go. They remind us, hopefully, to enjoy whatever one we're in. They remind us that they won't be sticking around indefinitely. I don't know what season of life you find yourself in right this moment, but allow me the pleasure of gently reminding you that we aren't in control, but there is Someone who has set the whole thing spinning and will hold us in his hand no matter where we find ourselves. And this season will be changing...maybe sooner than you think.

Ecclesiastes 3:1 There is a time for everything, and a season for every activity under heaven...

Fifty Two

Unexpected Gifts

I read a book while I was in Africa last year called <u>Gift of the Red Bird</u> (Paula D'Arcy). A friend had given it to me and I chose to bring it along because I wanted some light reading. I thought Africa would be tough enough to swallow so maybe some short, light essays would help to balance out my emotional state. I believe the book pretty much started with a car accident with the author losing her husband and child, while pregnant and also in the car (don't quote me on details). Needless to say, I was simultaneously drawn in and yet, as you can imagine, walking around with a heavy heart and nowhere to escape to. Still, a very good book.

I think of the phrase "gift of the red bird" quite often because of where I live. Which is in a breathtaking place that I sometimes still can't believe I get to call home. We're situated next to a county-preserved pond, surrounded by trees (eighty-two of which are in our yard, according to my son's counting). And there are two little patches of trees where I see a male cardinal, all year long. I don't know if it's the same one, or two separate ones who have searched out their own little corner of land, but just recently, I've told myself to take it as a reminder each and every time I see it/them flit from one tree to another that Jesus loves me. So simple but so effective.

I can be washing my hands at the kitchen sink, look out and see my red bird perched on top of the birdfeeder, or I can be sitting on my living room couch looking out at the pond and notice the red bird flying back and forth between a few small trees, and I will say, sometimes outloud and sometimes in my head, "Jesus loves you, Beth". And it works. It stops me in my tracks, maybe for only a few seconds, and it brings my heart back to its focus, to its center, to its ruler.

Jesus is my Lord, whether I think about him once a day or all day long…but I'm human…and I tend to flit myself from thing to thing, idea to idea, person to person. And I need to be reminded that he's there, all the time, right beside me, living in me, and so if a red bird is how I remember, well, that's a gift.

Fifty Three

I've Got My More-than-Enough

I have a lot of holes inside of me. Emotional and spiritual holes. Some I was born with, others developed because of things that have happened to me along the way, and some, to be honest, are holes I ripped open wide myself.

It's taken me a long time to embrace the word *needy* as a self-description. Who wants to say they are needy? *No one* as far as I can tell. But I am. And it's not just that I have needs, as does every person on the planet. But I've got some unmet ones. (Clearing throat…so do you.)

I have found over the years a myriad ways of trying to fill them up. I've been like the kid who stuck his thumb in the dam. I've used food, shopping, TV watching, computer surfing, people, just to name a few ways. But one can only do that for so long.

It's only maybe been the past year or so that I've actually figured out what my needs are, determined which ones tend to go unmet, and then took the long hard look inside to see how I've been inappropriately trying to meet them. Not pretty.

And it's only been in recent months when I realized how all these things fit together and how I do actually have a choice to break the patterns of how I try to unhealthily fill up those empty spaces inside.

And an even more recent revelation, as in *yesterday* --- maybe it's okay if I sit with the emptiness from time to time. Not every longing has to be met. What a concept.

So something I started praying, like yesterday, was that Jesus would truly become my enough. He already is, I just don't always let him be that for me. And that I would go to him for those things. And that, when those things still don't pan out the way I'd like (remember, it's promise fulfillment not wish fulfillment we're after), that I'll still be okay, and won't go running in a dangerous direction. Or seven. (What can I say, I'm so very human…)

Fifty Four

So Much More

Over the years, I've heard the argument against Christianity that it's just a bunch of old-fashioned rules and not much else.

Sure, the Bible suggests a few things we don't do, like, you know, kill each other and take each other's stuff. And there are some things it says we should do, like be kind to each other and help each other out. But it's so much more than do's and don'ts.

I think my favorite part about being a follower of Christ – and there are so many things I love about it – is that I get to tap into the spiritual side of life and of myself. Frankly, and I don't mean to sound judgy when I say this, I have no idea really how people live as if there is no God. What I mean by that is this…my life is so rich because of the realization that there is something, Someone, so much greater than I am, and that he invites me to be in relationship with him and to be a part of all he's got in store. It's simply amazing when you think about it.

In fact, I can't imagine really how in the world my life would've turned out if hadn't accepted Christ into my heart and life when I was fifteen. I mean, sure, I'd probably be married and have some kids. I'd probably have a house and maybe a job. But what depth would there be? What purposes? What adventures? What meaning? (And you can barely even get me started on what peace and comfort in difficult times? Where would I turn through all the hard stuff? No idea.)

Don't get me wrong. Life is a gift. Just plain old life. Seasons. Music. Books. Children. Friendship. Food. Holidays. Even shopping (had to throw that one in). There is so much out there that is fun and beautiful and cool.

But first of all, all those regular life things are enhanced, sort of like watching a movie with 3D glasses, when you live them out in light of an eternal perspective, when you get to do so while holding the hand of the One who created it all.

And sort of oppositely, in comparison, those regular life things are nothing stacked up next to the utter privilege of simply knowing God.

You know, we could have a Maker who just didn't bother bridging the gap between us, who ruled from a distance, who set us spinning and then didn't connect with us at all ever again. But the Bible and my experience tell me that's not the kind of Maker we have.

And I'm so, so grateful. Because my life is more full, more free, more beautiful, more abundant because I get to live it with him.

Fifty Five

Only Human

Three times within about twelve hours, I was reminded of my humanness. And when I say that, I don't mean my propensity to sin, I mean my physicality. That I am a physical being and that my body and what it can do and see and feel and hear and touch are an integral part of my human and spiritual experience.

It began with a moment that took me completely by surprise in church. We are in the middle of a series called "Return of the King" and the teaching pastor was talking about the new heaven and the new earth. These are things that I have heard sermons on and read about for years, but nothing delights my soul quite like envisioning the future. And here's the thing, it's not like I'm crossing my fingers that what the Bible says about eternity really is true. I believe it's true. And in case I doubted my own level of belief, I was given some unexpected reassurance. The pastor said something to the effect of, "If you're thirsty, you'll be able to drink from the River of Life. If you're hungry, you'll be able to eat from the Tree of Life." And I don't know why, but I began to cry. Not like sobbing crying or anything. But I had a physical response to those two sentences…my body reacted with relief because it was hearing promises…it was hearing something that I could count on and look forward to in my current weariness. There will be a day when I will no longer thirst and hunger, and I believe that so deeply that my tear ducts sprang to life at the mere mention of it.

Later that day, we had a holiday party at our home with about thirty members of family. I am an introvert. My idea of a good day is sitting on my couch with a book, a cup of tea, a blanket, a candle and gazing out the window. Like, for ten hours at a time. It's just the way I was created. I was created to be filled up emotionally, mentally, physically and spiritually by time alone, not by time in a large crowd. And I know this. So, there are some things I do to prepare myself for six hours of thirty people in my home. I had some time with Jesus. I took a nap. I did a few minutes of yoga. I even put four drops of some herb called Rescue Relief under my tongue as a supposed stress reliever. And then I took a deep breath and welcomed them into my home. About a half dozen things in those six hours made me uncomfortable. I felt like I was a filled up balloon that was not yet tied off, and every time something happened that I didn't like, a little more air was let out of me. Let me tell you, by the end of the evening, I was more physically and emotionally exhausted – depleted – than I had felt in ages. I physically felt the ramifications of how God had created me emotionally. And though I am so grateful to be an introvert and I love everything about it, I was painfully aware as the evening progressed how that can hinder me in a very physical way.

Then toward the end of the party, I asked my son to join me outside to collect all the candles that I had placed throughout our yard earlier in the day to welcome our family and make our yard a winter wonderland. And it was snowing with those big puffy snowflakes and yet, barely cold at all. I love those kinds of nights. And Jack and I stopped what we were doing and looked up into the night sky and watched hundreds of thousands of snowflakes slowly descend, "as if coming from nowhere", he said, and we caught them with our tongues and I even began to twirl. I was simply delighted by creation. And I physically and even emotionally began to feel better, to regain something I had been losing throughout the afternoon and evening. (It probably helped knowing the party was almost over, but still…) I was able to physically enjoy God and his gorgeous and fun creation of fluffy snowflakes that melt on your tongue.

I think I forget sometimes how interwoven my entire being is with itself. I'm not just a spiritual person who has to deal with a body or an emotional mess sometimes who remembers to bring God into how I'm feeling about something. It's all interrelated…it's all how God made me… it's all a part of the whole. And right now, that makes me smile, on my face and down into my soul.

Fifty Six

New

I've heard *insanity* defined as doing the same thing over and over again hoping for different results. Well, this year, I'm choosing to walk away, or at least go down with the ship trying, from my version of insanity.

Seems I've got some anger that I'm holding onto like Linus with his dirty little blanket. It's doing me no good but darnit if I don't love to drag it around with me. But not anymore. Or at least, I hope not anymore.

I'm trying something new today. I don't know if it'll work. But I'm putting myself out there and testing the waters and hoping that this new thing will help me in my desire to let joy overtake sadness and gentleness diffuse all this anger.

I realize that I can only do so much. I realize that a certain circumstance that seems to be my largest trigger isn't changing and might not ever change, so I can only do so much. But today, I'm doing all I can. I'm showing up. I'm hoping for a change. But if the change doesn't come, and it may not, that's okay too.

Because I can keep praying. And I can keep trying. And I can keep repeating my mantras. And I can cling to God even in this specific brokenness. And I can keep hoping that Jesus will do what I can't do, which is, basically, heal my own heart.

So here's to changing things we can…here's to trying new things when the old things stop working…here's to waiting and seeing…here's to healing and wholeness and joy and gentleness and more and more of Jesus.

Fifty Seven

Fear Not

Jesus said, "There is nothing to fear."
Luke 5:10a (The Message)

When I was journaling this morning, I wrote down five things that are on my mind today. Little things and big things.

Two nights in a row, I've been up in the middle of the night for about two hours. Hate that. This concerns me a bit, because I used to do this all the time and I don't want this pattern to return.

I'm starting to get my newest book out there just a bit. Testing the waters. I have never felt more unsure about something I've written then this thing. I don't know what kinds of responses to expect. Though I'm thinking things like "blech" and "stop writing". Maybe that's a girl thing.

A work thing with someone in my family just came up that's a little disconcerting.

A thought that I thought I let go of has resurfaced and it's getting under my skin. Unnerving to say the least. Like I can't control what comes into my head or something.

And then something that's been brought to my attention about my children and my parenting. I needed to hear it but I don't know what to do with it.

Then I read, after creating my list of woes, some words of Jesus. I spent Thanksgiving through Christmas leisurely reading Luke one and two to allow myself to ruminate on the Christmas story. And then I decided to keep right on reading in Luke because when was the last time I actually read one of the gospels? Yikes. So I'm in Luke 5 where Jesus has pushed himself out onto the lake in a boat to speak to the masses on the beach. And he has just told Simon to toss the net back in after a tough fishing day. And Simon doesn't want to but he does, out of respect or to be kind or to placate. And the net is full to overflowing and he drops to his knees in worship. And Jesus says to him, "There is nothing to fear."

But I just listed five things that are concerning me. Therefore, that are worrying me. Which really means I've got five things just this morning that I fear. I fear insomnia. I fear being tired every day. I fear that I cannot write to save my life. I fear no one will like this new thing. I fear this weird work situation. I fear this nagging thought. And I fear that I'm messing up my children.

But Jesus says, *there is nothing to fear.* Nothing. Not when he's in the picture. And he is in my picture.

So I laid it all down. I ran it through my little grid...what can I change, what can I do not a thing about, what do I have no idea how to handle? And I laid it down again. And then I praised God and thanked him that He is God and I am not, and I asked him for wisdom and to entangle some of these things.

Because today Jesus told me not to fear and today I'm choosing to obey.

Fifty Eight

Grateful Mess

I am a grateful mess. That phrase came to my mind today as I sat with the elements in my hand. I've been following Jesus for almost twenty four years which means I have more than likely taken communion, on this side of actually believing in him, around two hundred and fifty times. I am of the belief that you should only observe communion after entering into a personal relationship with Christ, if you're taking the thing seriously and reverently, and if you're not currently in a season of sin.

Well, in the past twenty odd years, I have taken it as a believer. Check. But in the past twenty odd years, I can tell you that I have not always taken it in reverence and holy wonder. Nor have I always been, clear throat, sinless. Let me explain what I mean by that. There are the daily sins that trip us up, that communion brings to the light in a sense, and we can look at and shed through asking of forgiveness and accepting the truth that Jesus took it on for us, and then there are the times when we're in habitual, private sin. I have taken communion during those times. In other words, there are times I've done it when I had no business taking it.

But what hit me this morning was beauty. There is a beauty in the ritual. There's beauty in the cycle, the rhythm, of another month going by (as our church does it) and looking back and realizing, as Matt Redmond's words reminded me today that...

And once again I look upon the cross where You died
I'm humbled by Your mercy and I'm broken inside
Once again I thank You
Once again I pour out my life

See, I was mid-self-beating-up. Oh, this darn thing that I can't shake. How I want to be different. How I want a clean slate. How each month I say to myself, this is the month. But here I am, once again pouring out my life, once again thanking God for taking my sin upon himself. And as I sat there, in a room of maybe two hundred other adults doing the same thing I was doing, I realized that once again, we were all coming back to him. Surely I'm not the only with things that hold me down that I can't seem to change, though there is progress and mercy and grace and growth, thankfully. But we were all, once again, one measly month later, back on our knees before God saying we need him again. Still.

A grateful mess. I'll be a mess as long as I'm taking a breath. And dear God, I pray, I'll be a grateful one for all of my days as well.

Fifty Nine

Lay it Down, for the Thousandth Time

I'm sitting here trying to figure out why I can't think of anything to write about right now. And why I haven't written anything since last Sunday. That's sort of odd for me. I just made myself look at my calendar for this past week to see what might've been going on.

I think I might know what it is…I've had a couple fairly intense conversations with my kids this week and they don't feel like they're for public consumption. Usually I write about practically everything in my life, hearts not just on my sleeve but hanging out all over because why not, and if there is something that's just too private, I couch it in metaphors and analogies.

But this week has just been too…real…intimate maybe. Hard to hear. And I can't share. And that is what my mind has been focusing on this week come to think of it. In fact, I'm tending this thing like a tomato plant, as a dear friend pointed out. Meaning, I'm worrying, and I'm feeding this worry with near-obsessive thoughts.

But I'm trying. I'm really trying to lay it down. Unfortunately, as soon as I lay the thing down, I think of one more aspect and I find myself hunkered down on the ground lying there next to it. Did it just move? Did it grow? Is that a new leaf? Wait, it wasn't that color green five minutes ago, was it? Is it poisonous? What should I do about it? Should I prune it, leave it alone, throw it out? You get my drift.

Oh, look at me…there I go couching in analogies again. I thought I wasn't going to do that this time around. But since I am, do I have any little gems to offer you? To those of you who may have a worrying gene or two in their body.

Let me think.

Well, this verse that I read yesterday unnerves me more than anything else. Luke 8:50 (The Message) says that "Jesus said, 'Don't be upset. Just trust me and everything will be all right.'"

This is one of those that I think to myself, "Okay. Yeah, I'll get right on that." Which, I know, is irreverently snarky and slightly faithless of me. I'm comforted and put off in one fell swoop. Only God's Word does this to me. So I read that, and write it in my journal, and feel slightly guilty that I already know I will fail at this one, and then I move on with my day.

So, then there's today's verse from Luke 9:11b (The Message) that said, simply, "Those who needed healing, he healed."

Oh. Like, I pretty much have nothing to do with it. I pretty much need to hand over my tomato plant and its burgeoning fruit and all that goes with it and, really, hand it over. I mean, I may have to do something about it eventually, but right now what I need to do with it is put it to prayer and wait. I'm not going to find the answer in the tomato plant, so tending to it and examining it really is just sucking precious life away from me. (How I wish I could remember this sentence in the moment…maybe the very next time, I actually will remember it.)

So, that's what I've got today. My version of *don't worry, be happy*, I guess, but with *trust Jesus* and *give it to him* thrown in.

Sixty

Supposed To

Yesterday would have been my eighteenth wedding anniversary. Had my husband, then-fiance, not broken our engagement, that is. That was my first, first-person heartbreak. Meaning, I had gone through being a child of divorce, but that was more about my parents than about me. So, this was my first, big, hard thing. And it was devastating.

But I was telling my son about it this morning, leaving out the devastating part, and I said to him, "Had we gotten married on January 25, 1992, when we were *supposed to* (please imagine me air-quoting feverishly right about now) instead of when we did, I wouldn't have had you. You wouldn't even exist." He gave me that look that tells me he totally doesn't know what I mean. But when I said those words while looking my sweet boy in the eyes, it took my breath away.

That devastation that I would've given anything not to live through back then brought me Sara and Jack. Because I'm sure that if we'd gotten married earlier, I would've started bugging Kevin about having kids earlier, and he would've relented earlier, and therefore we would've created altogether different human beings (well, *God* would have, but you know what I mean).

Side note: when I told Jack our actual wedding day and year, he didn't say anything for a moment (turns out he was calculating) and then he said, incredulously, "You waited another almost two years?" My response, "You are preaching to the choir, brother." (I got that quizzical look again.)

So if today is a day that you happen to be in the middle of a really hard thing and you can't catch a glimpse of the other side, or you have been through something that you thought would simply break you beyond repair and restoration, please allow my small story of deep pain to bring a bit of encouragement…a bit of a reminder…maybe even a bit of hope… that good things can and do and will come from hard things. In fact, I can't think of even one hard thing in my life that didn't produce at least one good thing that was better than the hard was hard.

So hang in there, *really*…and keep your eyes and heart open. You just might be surprised.

Romans 8:28 (The Message) That's why we can be so sure that every detail in our lives of love for God is worked into something good.

Sixty One

What My Love Can Do

Jack came home from school yesterday, walked in the door, and immediately realized he had forgotten his science book. His shoulders slumped and he got instantly upset (with himself, I'm assuming). He moved on though, set his book bag down, and started to unload it on the dining room table to get going on his other two assignments that he could complete. Then he realized he forgot his social studies book as well. That was too much for him. He walked away from the table and went straight into his room, shutting his door.

I sighed. I've seen this scenario play out before. I'd say at least once a week or so, he forgets something he needs to get his homework done. So, I let him stew for a little bit and then walked past his room and knocked on the door, asking if I could come in. Silence. *Can we talk?* Silence. *Okay, then. I love you and I'm sorry and I'm praying for you.* Silence. So I walked away.

Another 45 minutes later and I tried again, but with a different tactic. (Plus, come on…45 minutes?) I wrote a note that simply said "I love you" and slipped it under his door.

He wrote back within seconds. There was a stick figure of a boy with tears flowing down, and words that broke my heart. "It won't help!" Whoa. We kept the note-writing/note-slipping for a few minutes until I was finally allowed entrance.

But really…*whoa*. And really, he was right. My loving him wouldn't be able to help much. Because here's what my love can't do. It can't miraculously get his two needed books in his hands. It can't wave a magic wand and get his teachers to say, "No big deal, Jack." It can't take away his sadness. It can't make him remember something. It can't change his personality, make him more organized. It can't make all the kids like him, make him taller, make him feel less insecure. Though I probably would do all of those things with my love if I could.

But here's what it can do. Because love really is a powerful thing. My love can listen. My love can write a note and slip it under the door. My love can rub a back gently. My love can hand out Kleenex. My love can whisper some advice. My love can whisper a prayer. My love can believe in Jesus enough for the both of us when he doesn't still know yet if Jesus can be trusted. My love can laugh at his jokes and let him teach me dance moves from gym class and play the game of Life for the umpteenth time and pack a lunch and make a breakfast and remind him as often as I can that my love for him is real and that Jesus's love for him is even bigger and better.

Some homework got done last night. Most of it did not. My love couldn't do anything about that. But it drew him out of his room and helped him to come up with a plan for today, and even helped him laugh a little bit. My love could do that.

Sixty Two

All Quiet on the Western Front

I can hear the second hand ticking away on my office clock. It's pretty much that quiet in my house all day every day (well, 6:30am through 3:10pm, Monday through Friday, September through May – which is now).

I tend to love quiet. I just heard a great line in a movie I was watching last night…"what I would give for just a handful of quiet…" Okay, I don't tend to love quiet. I outright with-full-abandon love quiet.

But right now, things are too quiet. Things are quiet creatively for me. I just finished my first novel only to find out a day later, by doing a little tangential internet research, that novels are typically around 80,000 to 100,000 words long. Ummm, *o-kay*. So what I finished then was a novella, not a novel. I'd be okay with that except publishers apparently don't even give first glances at novellas. So, how do I take a book that I thought was done and, you know, double it? I don't know. No idea. Thus the creative quietness.

Things are quiet in an important relationship of mine where I had to speak the truth in love, say a very difficult thing, and now I am suffering on the quiet end of the silent treatment. This was predicted but it's not ever welcome. And it's driving me ever-so-slightly batty. Though I'm sticking to my guns because I have truth on my side and I did the right thing no matter how long the quiet lasts. But still, this kind of relational quiet can be an icky kind of quiet.

But then there's the good quiet. And I've got that going in spades right now, which, gratefully balances out the rest. I've got sweet moments with both of my kids the past few days…tender touches and knowing sighs and perfect words exchanged in person, via email, via texts from dear, dear friends yesterday and the day before…

And then there's Jesus. The way he swoops in to save the day sometimes is just beyond me. He and I have this thing with the Psalms. Now, I'm not recommending this as a really great theological tool to find the answers to all your problems, but it helps me. A lot. If I'm stuck or sad or blah or angry, I'll hold my Bible in my hand and say something like, "Got anything for me right now?" and a number will come to mind. And I go to that Psalm. And nine times out of ten it's spot on for what I'm going through or feeling and it brings quiet reassurance that the God of the universe knows. You know…*knows*. Knows me. Knows my heart. Knows my circumstance or predicament or rock and a hard place that I inevitably, continually find myself fin. He knows. This is the good kind of quiet.

So, I love quiet. Even when it's hard and fuzzy and frustrating. Because in the quiet, I can hear what's most important.

Sixty Three

Real Life

I sat in church this morning with a heavy heart, with a burden on my mind, but I did my best to fully engage in worship with as much joy as I could muster up. Then I went on to do my best to track with my pastor as he told us how Jesus chose to be a servant.

And then I looked around the auditorium and I realized, yet again, that I was not the only person with something weighing me down. It was as if I saw one of those cartoon conversation bubbles over each person's head and they were filled with things like, "I just lost my job two days ago," and "my teenage daughter is pregnant," and "my fourteen year old decided to get drunk last weekend," and "my husband hits me," and "my wife is leaving me". Yes, gasp, *in the church.*

We put on a show. We walk in, take our seats, engage in orderly worship, sit still and keep our mouths shut during a well-packaged service, then we walk out, maybe get a cup of coffee or exchange pleasantries and keep on walking to our cars, heading back home to our lives. Our real lives. Our lives that may be completely messed up, completely out of control, utterly hanging on by a thread.

And maybe we have to. Maybe there's no room or no space for us to be rip-open-our-hearts real on a Sunday.

But, Lord, I hope every person in auditoriums across the country this morning who went home to a real life that is unimaginably difficult is clinging to you and has at least one someone that they can share it all with. Because if they don't have you and if they don't have a friend, I don't know how they will get through whatever they're having to get through.

Sixty Four

Where You Go, I Will Follow

This following Jesus thing can be tricky sometimes. There are many, many *don'ts* in the Bible that help me know what to steer clear of…lying, adultery, slander, malice, worry, yada yada yada. And there are many, many *do's* that guide me in what I should do…pray, believe, serve, hope, love, et cetera.

But then there are some areas in life that the Bible does not have a specific bullet-pointed list for. Where you should go to college. If you should marry John Smith. Take the job in Akron or in Beloit. You catch my drift.

I'm in one of those places, sort of. I've made a decision based on prayer, wise counsel (immense amount of wise counsel), what I know of God's character, some random circumstances here and there, and a few whispers from Jesus. I feel as confident as I can feel about something like this. Because the thing is…scandalous, for lack of a better word.

I'm standing up for myself in a way that I never have before. I am changing the steps of the dance, no longer waltzing but enjoying hip hop, as a friend put it. And though I'm as sure as I can be, things feel fuzzy, grey. Time is moving in slow motion. My heart is adjusting to the new rhythm but my tummy still has butterflies. I spoke the truth in love and, surprise surprise, it wasn't taken all that well.

But I'm learning a couple things along the way. I cannot predict or control someone's response to my felt obedience. But even when the response is not so great, or downright ugly, I must still stay the course. I must not let words or actions that throw me for a loop actually throw me for a loop. I am doing what I feel Jesus has led me to do, and he already sees the outcome. So I don't have to know it or worry about it or obsess about it, hypothetically of course.

I'm also learning that sometimes it's okay to be scandalous. I've worked out the worst-case scenarios and, guess what, none of them scare me anymore. I think I used to be easily intimidated, but something in me has shifted and I have a respectful bring-it attitude.

Because if I feel like I'm truly following the leading of God, and I truly do, then what can man do to me? Not a thing. Not a single thing. *Eyes on Me, baby*, I heard Jesus say.

So that's where my eyes will be.

Sixty Five

In Crisis

Lucinda McDowell in <u>Spa for the Soul</u> says, "There are three possible outcomes of any crisis: a change for the better, a change for the worse, or a return to the previous level of functioning. Most of us desire that the outcome is for the better but do we realize that much of that depends on our own attitude? The Chinese term for crisis (*weji*) is made up of two symbols – one for 'danger' and one for 'opportunity'. The English word is taken from the Greek word *krinein*, meaning 'to decide'. So, every time of crisis is a time of decision. Yes, it is dangerous, but it is also an opportunity."

I've been living in a state of emotional crisis for as long as I can remember. It courses through my veins and, sadly, I don't think my body or mind know what to do with a state of equilibrium when it peeks through in slivers.

But this is what I know, crisis or not. God has shown himself to be faithful and true to me in the past few days in ways I could never have imagined.

He parted some waters that were rough indeed. He sent wise counsel in the form of deeply caring friends. He sent support – emotional, physical, spiritual – in the form of those same friends. He whispered next steps and sent me Psalms (specifically 56, 91 and 116) at the moment I needed them, one a day, each the perfect Psalm on just the right day.

And now I sit on the somewhat other side and I talk to myself with this, from Psalm 116:7:

Be at rest once more, O my soul, for the LORD has been good to you.

My soul is fighting to be at rest…it doesn't want to be yet…but my Lord *has* been good to me, deeply good, and so I will continue to remind myself of that until it quiets itself down, even if it takes a long while.

May my attitude embrace the opportunity that is before me to heal and to grow even stronger, even if I don't want to quite yet.

Sixty Six

One Seed, One Part

I've said it before and I'll say it again. I love what I do. In part because I cannot believe that a) God lets me do this, and b) that I actually love it because I used to hate it. What I'm talking about is public speaking… getting up in front of a bunch of women and sharing my stories and experiences and truths that God has impressed upon me through His Word and through my life. I love it. I love the during part and I love the after part. Because the after is when I get to talk to women one-on-one.

Today was no exception. Today found me in Racine, Wisconsin at a church I'd never been to before. I didn't even know how they found out about me to invite me but it turns out that a gal that attends a local group that I've spoken at about five or six times has a sister in the group I was at today and she recommended me. So sweet.

So I did my talk on friendship where I touch on our relationships with other women, with our husbands and with God, where I remind us that we're created for coming alongside each other and coming alongside God, and then I headed out to the lobby.

To be honest, sometimes, this is hands-down the most awkward time for me. Sometimes I just sit at my book table with not a soul coming up to me to talk or look at my books. I reassure myself in these times that God already knew this, that it's not about me, that no one must need to talk or pray, and then I usually pray for the women I just spoke to while they chit-chat with each other or make their craft (or I doodle). But today, I had several come up to me to share. And a couple of them had a catch in their voices while they did.

Two in particular caught my attention and I asked if I could pray with them (favorite, favorite part of what I do…because that's the most eternal thing I do all day). One gal mentioned being overwhelmed, sad, her kids were driving her crazy. So of course I prayed with her – for peace, for strength, for divine measures of patience, and that Jesus would draw her close.

And then I was packing my stuff up as I needed to get on the road to be home from Wisconsin before my kids walked through the door at the end of the day, and this precious woman walked up to my table and said, "I've lived here for four years. I'm moving in June. I don't have any real friends. I don't think anyone will miss me when I leave. And I don't even get any of this faith stuff." I stood up, walked around to the other side of the table and she said, "I know you have to leave…I'm sorry for coming up at the last minute…" And I looked her in the eyes and said, "You might be the only reason I even came here today," and she started to cry and I gave her a hug and let her cry on my shoulder. You know us girls…the whole time all she could do was apologize for crying, "I never cry in public," she kept saying. "It's okay," I kept whispering.

Then this was my "please give me words quick, Holy Spirit" advice to this sweet gal. "First of all, I think you'll be surprised at whether or not you'll be missed. But keep coming back here and try to get connected even in this short time. And as far as faith goes…I don't want to try to force something on you that you're not ready for…" And then I glanced up and saw the group leader standing ten feet away, ready and willing to step in, so I motioned for her to come over, and continued, "Do you two know each other? She was just telling me that she has some questions about the whole faith thing and though I'd love to just pray the prayer with her right here and now, I bet you will be able to give her the time she needs." The leader nodded enthusiastically. The sweet lady stood next to me with tears streaming down her cheeks, and I asked if I could pray. So I prayed. Not "thee" prayer…not the prayer of salvation that guarantees she's locked in… though I wanted to. But I knew it wouldn't have been right. It would've been forced. I would've been running ahead, and sadly, just maybe, in part, so I could say that the Kingdom had been built today.

So I stepped aside. And I packed up my things and I watched the leader and this gal walk into another room to talk. And I drove away. And

I realized that I had just played my part. I planted a seed when I drove up to Wisconsin, leaving my family for the night (my son actually tearing up when I said goodbye). I planted a seed when I shared with the larger group of women how Jesus is my best friend, how I love him so. I planted a seed when I connected those two women. I planted a seed when I prayed with them. And then I handed the seeds over to the leader to continue the process when I walked away. I played my part. And I'm so glad there was someone else ready and willing to play hers.

Which begs the question, are you playing yours?

Sixty Seven

Knows Something I Don't Know

My one and only real neighbor lives on three acres of land. She tends to it nine months out of the year, letting winter run its course with only her shoveling her driveway to help it along. And today I saw her out and about doing what she does. She walks around. I've lived here for a couple years now and I have watched her walk around her yard, in the morning and in the evening, daily, taking stock, I suppose.

I must be honest here. I'm kind of judgmental about it. I don't do yard work. I don't garden. I wouldn't know the difference between two trees if they had labels on them. So I know I shouldn't judge, but here is what I'm thinking as I watch her.

Why do you do that? Your property is so tucked back off the road and you live by yourself and you have few visitors that, frankly, only you and sometimes us know what you even do in and to your yard, let alone see any difference. Why do you walk around with a, ummm…big pair of scissors (I'm sure it's called something else)…and cut branches off? You have, like, three hundred trees. No one will notice. It won't make a difference if you trim that branch or not.

Harsh, I know. But, it's not like I walk up to her and say these things…I just think them when I'm in my kitchen eating potato chips and happen to see her with her big scissors cutting off another random branch.

And then today I thought that maybe God is like my neighbor and I am like her yard. Maybe he walks around me, circles me, gives me a once-over, and then does it again, always looking, always searching for that branch that doesn't need to be there, that twig that could be picked up off the ground, that flower bush that would look more beautiful in a few months if only it were trimmed back. Maybe people look at my life sometimes and wonder why God is doing what he's doing in and to and through me. Maybe they wonder if it will ever make a difference. Maybe they wonder why he bothers.

I may not know why my neighbor does what she does. And it may not mean anything to me. But I bet, if her yard had feelings, it would be grateful that she tends to it with such intimate care. And I bet that it means something of deep value to her when she's able to bring a sprig of roses in, that she helped bring to life and flourish, and put them in a place of prominence in her home, where she can soak up its beauty.

Just like I'm grateful that my Father tends to me so intimately and just like I hope that parts of my life that he's paid special attention to bring beauty to my surroundings as well, even if the tending hurts or doesn't make sense to anyone else.

Sixty Eight

Heart

I've been thinking a lot about my heart lately. A lot. I've heard it said time and again that we're made up of mind, soul and spirit. And yet, I've never heard one single sermon on this. I can think of plenty of sermons on the body and how we treat it and what we had better make sure we keep it from doing. I can think of messages on my mind and garbage in, garbage out, and how I need to take thoughts obedient to Christ. But the heart? The soul? The spirit? Ummm, nope. Can't think of a one.

I actually Googled the question, "What is the difference between the soul, the heart, the spirit and the mind?" and here's what I got, from Tony Capoccia of Bible Bulletin Board:

"To show how important it is to know which Greek word is being use to gain a proper understanding, look at {this} verse: "Love the Lord your God with all your heart and with all your soul and with all your strength and with all your mind...." [Luke 10:27]. The word for "heart" here is "kardia" = "the thoughts or feelings." It does not refer to the flesh of the heart that pumps blood, but really our "mind" in the sense of our "soul" or "spirit." The word translated "soul" in the verse is "psuche" (breath). But the word translated "mind" here is not referring to our "soul or spirit" for the Greek word used is "dianoia" which refers to our "deep thoughts" that is, the exercise of our minds. So the verse used "heart and soul" for emphasis, since they really refer to the same thing: the "spirit," and then adds that we are to love our God with our actual thoughts."

So, it sounds to me like heart/soul/spirit are the same and mind is something separate. Good to know. With that said, allow me continue.

So I'm thinking about my heart. For two reasons. One, I've been having palpitations on and off for the last two months and I've never, ever had anything like this before. I even had an EKG and wore a holter monitor for twenty four hours. They found nothing but the flutterings, as I prefer to call them, are unsettling to say the least.

And two, my heart is hardening up. Not across the board, but on one certain subject I am practically numb. And I don't know how to change what I feel deep down in my heart/soul/spirit. I'm praying against coldness settling in. I'm acting, to the best of my ability, as if it's not...you know, trying the old adage of "fake it until you make it"...but "everything in me is drawing in, closing in around this pain" to quote Sara Groves, and I don't know how to fight against it.

So my heart, this paradoxically strong muscle that keeps me alive and yet fragile cavity that holds my deepest longings, is on my mind these days. I'm trying to tend to it, take care of it, pray healing over it (both physically and spiritually), pray for it to stay wide open when it wants to clench up and stay that way, guard it as Scripture commands, but the heart is a powerful and mysterious thing, and I'm just a girl who's a little weary these days.

Psalm 27:8
My heart says of you, "Seek his face!" Your face, LORD, I will seek.
Psalm 27:14
Wait for the LORD; be strong and take heart and wait for the LORD.

Sixty Nine

Sweep Away

This is what I learned this week. I think there might come a point in time when you are in too much pain to think clearly. In fact, you might not even know you're in that much pain until you look back, hindsight being 20/20 and all.

Well, this has been one of those weeks for me. I'm in some pain, grappling with some sadness, some anger, some fear, some hopelessness. Can I just say, though, that this is part of what I love about being a follower of Jesus? I can write that last sentence and know that it's all going to be okay, that *I'm* going to be okay, because "he who holds the last hour has assured us that everything will be glorious in the end." {Ben Patterson, <u>He Has Made Me Glad</u>}

But this has been a hard week - a hard stretch actually - and I've had to make quite a few decisions. Some were not that involved, some I was given direct counsel on, some were big and scary. And some, I messed up. That was part of my hard week this week. Someone said to me that I'm my own worst enemy right now and someone else suggested that I may just be so stuck that my perceptions are skewed. Both could very well be the case. (At least I'm open to sitting with these observations, something that I wouldn't have been willing to do even a year or so ago.)

There's a phrase that's been ringing in my ears this week – "force solutions". Yep, that's what I've been doing…forcing solutions. I've gotten impatient with the waiting on other people and the waiting on my God, so I've taken some matters into my own hands and promptly screwed them up. (*How old am I?*)

So I'm moving into this week with one mandate and one prayer (okay, about a thousand prayers, but this is a new one added into the mix). The mandate is this: *Think first.* The prayer is this: *Clear away the cobwebs, Lord. Help me see reality for what it is and then help me act appropriately.*

Neither the mandate nor the prayer guarantee successful choices or a successful week, but both definitely give me a better shot of not getting myself in above my head again. *I hope.*

Seventy

Cut and Run or Barrel on Through

It has recently been suggested to me that because of a certain relational issue that I've been dealing with for awhile now, that my testimony and Kingdom-building effectiveness are being affected.

Hmm.

Well, sure, on one hand, if I didn't have this thing in my life, I bet I would feel a heck of a lot more free. There'd be more light coming out of me and therefore I might be attracting more people to want to live life following Christ.

Then again, what is the alternative? Hole up until the thing's all better or all gone? Might never happen. Seriously. So, just hand back my talents to the Master when I see him at the end of this run and say, "Well, you saw what I had to deal with and I just figured 'my thing' would be a detriment, so I packed it up midway through…I was banking on you being totally okay with that…"

I don't think he would be.

So I keep moving, albeit more slowly then I used to, more guardedly because I don't want to mess things up out of my current pain. They say *hurt people hurt people* and I'm a hurtin' right now. So, I'm tentative. I'm trying to be appropriately honest with my inner circle and with those I'm attempting to serve. I'm taking some breaks while I fill up and heal up, letting Jesus cover me with a blanket, as a dear friend put it. But I'm still moving forward.

Case in point. I just said yes to something that is, like, exactly up my alley…exactly what I've been really wanting to do for a couple years but didn't think was even an option.

Do you know what this does for my soul? It shouts, "This is your redemption, baby!" And right now, in the middle of my thing, I could use a little redemption to light my way out.

Seventy One

Challenge and Hope

I'm not a fan of corny church signs.

"God doesn't believe in atheists, therefore, atheists don't exist."

"Our church is prayer conditioned."

"Exposure to the Son may prevent burning."

"Forget Batman! Come meet a REAL SUPER HERO."

"Try Jesus - if you don't like Him, the devil will take you back."

But I saw one the other day that struck me…it actually wasn't one of those goofy sayings, but announcing an upcoming sermon title.

Jesus, Our Challenge and Our Hope.

It struck me because I thought to myself, *Yep, Jesus is my hope. My only real, live, going-to-get-me-through-anything hope. Totally get that.*

But then I thought, *My challenge? How is that supposed to cheer me up?*

Maybe it wasn't supposed to cheer me up. Maybe it was supposed to get me thinking. Yes, Jesus is my hope. And I embrace that. Because it's happy. It's inspiring. It's optimistic. It's silver lining kind of talk. It's a balloon lifting me up and out. It's a "there's more to this life" reminder. It's, well, hopeful.

But I don't want to be challenged. I don't want hopeful Jesus to challenge me. I want Jesus to wipe away my tears, tell me everything's going to be alright, kick some butt and take names on my behalf, and then buy me a cookie. I don't want him to wipe away my tears, tell me it's all going to get harder before it gets better, that, by the way, it won't truly be better for about fifty years (i.e. when I'm on the other side), that I have to love those who I wish he'd take vengeance on, and that, oh yeah, I've got a lot of changing to do on my own and better stop pointing fingers.

(Apparently, I'd like to hear sermons called *Jesus, Our BFF and Our Hope.* Or *Jesus, Just Like a Fluffy Kitten.* Or *Jesus, Better than Shopping and Chocolate.*)

But that's not the Jesus I follow. I follow a Jesus who shows me the long view. Who reminds me who I am in him. Who comforts me in my pain, chastises me in my sin, calls me to a higher plane of thinking and living. Who provides me with an eternal hope and challenges me to not stay the same.

And if I'm honest…I crave both the hope and the challenge deep down into my bones.

Seventy Two

The Power of Words

I am one ticked-off mom right now. Three days in a row, my son has come home with a tale of being called another not-so-good name (from two different kids), and I'm sick of it. I'm angry. I'm sad. I want to go rip their arms off. Very Jesus-y of me, no?

Today my sweet boy was told to, "Shut up, loser". That was the mildest of the three. This would anger you even more if you knew Jack. He's got about the sweetest spirit ever. I was just thinking about him earlier today...a year or two ago, I had given him and his sister some money specifically to give away, for the exercise of it, and he wanted to give it to his five-year-old friend, Carter, in case he needed another heart surgery. Yes, this is the kid who is getting called names.

So I saw him come sulking up the driveway today off the bus and went out to shoot hoops with him to try and pry the story out of him. (Little tip: it worked.) Well, I asked questions and listened, and then gave my mom peptalk.

"Jack, sometimes kids are just plain mean. Not always, but sometimes. Be kind to the ones who are kind to you. And be respectful but don't engage those who are not." Then I started revving up a bit, I could tell, and I let my righteous anger do the talking.

"Who are you?" I asked him.

"Jack," he said.

"And who loves you?" I asked.

"Jesus," he answered.

"Who else?" I asked.

"You," he said.

"Are you smart?"

"Yes."

"Are you funny?"

"Yes."

"Are you kind?"

"Yes."

"Are you loved?"

"Yes."

"Then don't forget it," I finished, swooshing the ball into the basket. (Just kidding --- totally missed, but it sounded like a better basketball-peptalk kind of ending.)

And don't you forget it either. No matter what anyone else may say to you – including that darned voice in your head – *you are loved*. Completely and perfectly, to the moon and back. Let the power of true words overtake the power of hurting words each and every time, until they lose their power. *Swoosh*.

Seventy Three

Laying it Down

I'm seeing someone new. No, I'm not *dating*. A new counselor. And what this new counselor didn't know about me yet, but surely does now, is that I'm the teacher's pet. Always have been, always will be. So at the end of our first session, I said, while gleefully clapping, "Give me assignments!" He smiled, "Well, you're doing everything I would've told you to do, so... ummm...okay, read Psalm 91 each day." "Got it," I said. "And since you like to write, maybe write a happily-ever-after short story for this certain situation," he added. "Alright, I can try that," I said. "Oh, yeah, and *forgive*," he finished.

Picture a balloon being popped and the air slowly leaking out and it pathetically falling to the ground. "Ummm, I thought I had forgiven," I said, somewhat sheepishly.

"Well," he replied kindly, "show me an angry person and I'll show you someone who hasn't forgiven," he said.

I believe I said, "Ouch," at that point, but said I'd try to do that too. Teacher's pet, remember?

So I was sharing this interaction with my mentor, Charlotte (you all need a Charlotte — have I said that before?!), and she said, "Ooo, I can totally help you with that!" Her turn to be giddy with excitement. So she gave me two lists to write. List one: all current grievances. *No problemo on that one.* And list two: all expectations I have of this situation. *Alright,* I thought, *simple enough.*

The grievance list came pouring out of me as if I'd been punctured. But I apparently didn't know what she meant by an expectation. She meant, things I am hoping for. But what I wrote was a list of my realities...

because, it turns out, I've stopped hoping. So she sent me back to the drawing board to write a list of hopes – can I just say, *harder than you'd think!!* – and she and I scheduled a date to meet at a beautiful chapel in a sweet little town.

First of all, this place is steeped in history and beauty. This was the third time I'd been there. The first time was about a year ago, to celebrate finishing going through the twelve steps with Charlotte. The second time was to pray with a dear friend before going out for tea. And then today.

God was gracious in protecting that space during the forty-five minutes we were there from anyone else just walking in off the street. Charlotte started us off with a responsive reading of Psalm 136 ("...his love endures forever...") and prayed for our time, and led me up to the front for us to kneel before the Lord and the cross.

She told me to read off each of my lists (three pages worth) slowly and as if I were placing each hurt, each wound, each sad, met *and* wishful-thinking, unmet expectation into the hands of Jesus, at the foot of the cross, reminding me that he had died to kill sin.

Then, she boldly instructed me to walk to the altar and lay myself face and body down on the floor for a few moments of silent reflection. (I trust her this much.) The entire time I was just asking Jesus to help me truly let it all go, to truly forgive through and through.

She then said, "Elisabeth, get up in the name of the Lord." (Breath-taking, right?) Then she walked me to where the cross was, I folded my sheets of paper up and I placed my lists underneath the cross, where she prayed for me again.

Do I feel different? Yes and no. Yes, today was a line-in-the-sand kind of day. Today I told Jesus I would hold onto these things no longer. But no, in that I physically feel the same, and no, in that I know that I'm going to have to let it all go again and again, even later today.

But forgiveness is an interesting thing. When I let it go, I'm not letting it go into oblivion, into the universe, I'm letting it go onto Jesus. I'm taking my offender off my hook and not just placing this person on the ground but lifting them up and onto God's great and mighty hook. And after I do so, I get on my knees in humility because, as Beth Moore says, "when the mighty arm of God's justice comes sweeping by, I want to make sure I am out of its way."

Forgiveness is not about the other person. It's not about okaying a wrongful action, or a string of them. It's not contingent on an apology. Or even on the action stopping. It's one hundred percent for my sake. It's one hundred percent about my freedom. Because, as Beth Moore also says, "you can't hold onto your anger and your first love at the same time," and my precious Jesus knows I want to be holding onto him more than anything else in this world.

So with everything in me, I will let go.

Seventy Four

Captive

Someone recently called me on the fact that I have running-wild negative thoughts. *And...*, I thought. *Who doesn't?* Well, so it seems, not like I do. So I was challenged to write down each of my thoughts into two columns – *sinful* and *uplifting*. I took on the challenge...or I should say, I attempted to take on the challenge, making two columns in my journal and placing it on the dining room table, with the plan to stop and record each thought whenever I had one.

Umm, here's the thing. I apparently have these rampant thoughts, like, all the time. In the shower. On my run. While driving. While vacuuming. While applying mascara. I stood next to my journal at the dining room table and said, outloud to no one, "I won't get anything else done today!" So I decided not to do that list-making thing.

But I appreciated the idea and still knew I had work to do in the taking-my-negative-thoughts-captive arena, so the Spirit brought something to mind.

I've heard it hundreds of times before that if I were the only person alive, Jesus loved me so much that he still would've gone to the cross to die just for me. But the flipside of that amazing grace-filled coin hit me like a ton of bricks...if I were the only person alive, Jesus would have *had* to go to the cross to die just for me, because my sin would have been enough to send him there.

So I determined that with each negative thought that crossed my mind about someone or something, I would say to myself...to Jesus...in my head or outloud if I were alone, "*I* sent You to the cross." And I'd repeat that phrase until the negative train of thought was derailed. I have gone on to add, in the past two weeks of trying this and saying this probably a thousand times, "*I sent You to the cross…and I am sorry…and I am grateful.*"

So just now, I was lying in bed, unable to fall asleep, and my mind started wandering down that negative thought trail again, and I said to myself this time, "I sent you to the cross…my anger sent you to the cross…my negativity sent you to the cross…my lying sent you to the cross…my critical spirit sent you to the cross…my judgmental attitude sent you to the cross…my hateful thoughts sent you to the cross…" And on and on I was able to continue, until I wasn't thinking that negative thing anymore. And until I was humbled once again.

As a woman, I tend to compare the worst of me to the best in other women. But I think I just might be as guilty, if not more guilty, of comparing my best to other people's worst in a pathetic attempt to puff myself up, and I'm tired of it. There are only two people that I should be comparing myself to…the me I was yesterday and the Savior that I am aspiring to become more like. And I shouldn't be judging anyone, even myself.

I *did* send Jesus to the cross…but with equal truth I must re-remind myself that he loved me enough to willingly go there for me, sin and all.

Seventy Five

Rest

It's 27 degrees and snowing right now. But it's that perfect 27 degrees and that perfect snow. Mild and slow and you can only hear the birds and pretty much nothing else and it's somehow not cold. So, I sat outside on a bench in my yard and took it all in.

Until my cat arrived and snuggled on my lap. He is an active snuggler. For the life of me, I could not get that thing to just settle down.

I wrapped my arms around him. I stroked his back gently. I whispered, "It's okay. Just sit still. Let me hold you. You can just rest. Shhhh…"

And then my intimate Heavenly Father impressed upon me that I remind him of my cat. How I struggle even in his arms. How all he wants me to do is sit still and quiet my heart and rest for awhile.

In fact, he doesn't just want me to rest in his arms for my own good --- though, trust me, he does because he knows it really does do me deep good --- but he wants me to rest in him for his own good.

I was reminded in those quiet moments with my squirrelly cat on my lap that I make life so hard. That God created me for his pleasure. That when God looks at me, he smiles. And maybe sighs at all my fits and starts. That every day he is whispering to me, "It's okay. Just sit still. Let me hold you. You can just rest. Shhhh… I love you…"

If only I'd slow down and quiet down enough to hear and to believe.

Seventy Six

A Pill

I am not easy to get along with. My closest girlfriends and my mother may disagree, but I have offended more people in this life of mine than, well, probably than you have in yours. I'm not one of those people that everybody loves. And I'm not one of those people who's never met a stranger, or however that saying goes. I'm an octagon of rough edges.

So there is a passage in Scripture that is the bane of my existence and yet I have practically set up shop in. *Matthew 18.* In fact, I used to do this so often, being on staff at a church and offending people left and right, that I turned it into a verb; as in, "I have to Matthew 18 Joe..." or "I just got Matthew 18'd again..."

Let me refresh your memory in case you're one of those people who has never had this joy-filled experience:

Verses 15-17 (Message) say, *"If a fellow believer hurts you, go and tell him—work it out between the two of you. If he listens, you've made a friend. If he won't listen, take one or two others along so that the presence of witnesses will keep things honest, and try again. If he still won't listen, tell the church. If he won't listen to the church, you'll have to start over from scratch, confront him with the need for repentance, and offer again God's forgiving love."*

Yep, good times.

Well, I had to Matthew 18 someone this week and I was dreading it with a capital D. I had no desire to do this but I knew I had to...I knew almost immediately that I had to confront this person. It didn't help that this person and I haven't had the easiest of relationships for several years now. But this person, who is a fellow believer, hurt me, so according to Matthew 18, I had to go and talk about it and attempt to work the thing out. Yuck. Sometimes the Bible just makes me mad. In fact, I was so mad that I told this verse to a friend who was praying me up and said, "But I don't want to end up friends!" You know, because I'm a ten-year-old.

So I went. I did the thing. I told this person very specifically how I was hurt. And not only did I not get an apology, but I got justified actions tossed my way. Excellent. *Now what,* I'm thinking. Well, I've Matthew 18'd enough to know that it's not about the results, that God holds the results. So we talked a little bit more, went a bit deeper, and then this person blew me away.

"You've held me at arm's length for years. You've shown me no respect, no love. I've leaned into your family and tried to love you and you have rebuffed all my attempts. *I cannot win with you.*"

Whoa. Now we're talkin'.

With tears in my eyes, I replied, "First of all, thank you so much for your vulnerability. Secondly, you're right. I have not shown you the respect you deserve. You have not done anything to deserve my unkindness and disrespect, and I am so sorry. Will you forgive me?" And with tears looking back at me, I was offered forgiveness.

Keep in mind, I went in for one entirely different objective, and came out healed. Funny what happens when you bother obeying God. In case you're wondering, he totally surprises you. And yes, that person and me, we're now friends.

Seventy Seven

Digging Around in the Past

A friend of mine from high school once told me I was nostalgic. For some very odd reason, I took it as a slam. I think at the time I thought she meant that I held onto the past or lingered back there as opposed to living life in the here and now. I never asked her to clarify, so I don't know her motives, but I realize that she was right. I am nostalgic in the best sense of the word and in the worst sense of the word.

I love to soak in memories of really sweet times and be grateful for the gifts in my life: good nostalgia. But I also can be a bit of a curmudgeon, turning into one of those grouchy old ladies, where I rehearse and rehash all the wrong that's been done to me: bad nostalgia.

Last week, I was driving through town and caught a glimpse of a car that is the same color, make and model of the car of an old friend. More accurately, a friend from my past that is no longer my friend. My eye immediately went to the license plate to see if it were her personalized one. Of course, it wasn't, but it struck me that TEN YEARS LATER, I still look for her plates. (As if I'd turn my car around and chase her and beg her to tell me what I did wrong to tank our friendship...not that I've ever fantasized about that or anything.)

But this time was different. Because this time I was literally in the middle of listening to a sermon on forgiveness. So I just told Jesus right then and there that I had messed up that friendship and that I was sorry. But that she had hurt me too. That I had done everything I could think of to reconcile it, but reconciliation takes two, and apparently I hadn't meant enough to her for her to make the effort. I told Jesus that even that part of it grieved my heart. I then begged him to help me finally let this darn thing go, to fully forgive her, and to not look for her license plates anymore.

Here's where he got all God on me. Later that same day, my daughter and I were working on a school project about her family, and we were rummaging through old pictures. In that pile I came across a picture of something very, very kind that past friend had done for me all those years ago. I asked God right then and there to make that small memory the thing I think about when she comes across my mind. That I no longer think of the hurt and what feels still so unresolved, but that I think of that one memory. Sort of like being able to choose your absolute best photo as your driver's license picture instead of the one they force upon you. I changed my picture, changed the image. How good of God to meet me in my request of a ten-year-old hurt all in the same day.

But it gets better, as only God could do. I ran into that friend literally that night. And I walked up to her and I said hello and I told her that I stumbled upon a picture of that act of kindness she had done for me and I thanked her again and told her how much it meant to me. She looked at me with a bit of dislike masked behind her smile, but I gave that to Jesus. And then I walked away knowing that God had healed a deep wound in me that day, all in that one day, all because I gave something up to him and invited him into it. *Only God.*

Seventy Eight

It Matters

I have some friends who are in the process of adopting their second child from Africa (they have two biological children and one child from Ethiopia). They are waiting on the court date of their daughter from Burkina Faso. They have had this court date postponed two times this month and so they invited a handful of friends and family over to their house last night to pray.

We reminded God who he is by reading Scripture and praying it back to him. We reminded him how much the fatherless mean to him and his promise to place the lonely in families. We prayed and cried and pleaded for his hand to move, for mountains to be pushed back, for nothing to block the court date from happening today.

Today, here are a few things that are true:

God is sovereign. He really is.

The court date didn't happen today. Again. Third time now. Postponed another two weeks. Hard to believe.

Asking matters. It really does.

It matters that we came together last night. It matters that this couple wants to welcome a girl into their family that they haven't met yet because they feel it's what God wants them to do and because they love the beauty of the picture that adoption paints of God's redeeming love for us. It matters that we prayed hard and that their other children saw it. It matters that we poured our hearts out because each time we open our mouths in prayer, I believe God smiles and we reaffirm that we, in fact, do believe in his goodness. It matters because we need to remember that he gives only good gifts...that his will, even though ridiculously hard to swallow sometimes, is for the best, even if we can't see it. It matters because every time we speak truth outloud the darkness hushes and quivers.

There is a darkness in this world but he who is in us is much greater than he who is that darkness.

Seventy Nine

Pouring Out

I have a friend who has wanted something for a very long time. She has surrendered her desire and has been transformed and healed and filled up and faithful all in the laying down. And now, she is mothering two sweet little girls for one week as part of an amazing program called Safe Families. She is pouring out and she is being poured into. Joy filled her face when I saw her with those girls.

I have a son who loves basketball, loves God and wanted to do something to change the world. So he wrote an email and asked some people for pledges and spent an hour shooting free throws – much harder than he anticipated – and raised enough money to purchase over 12,000 meals. He had a sore arm, he was sweaty, he was out of breath. He wanted to stop, he wanted to keep just a bit of the cash. (No worries, I wouldn't let him.) He poured himself out, he sacrificed a morning and a whole lot of energy, and the look of contentment on his face when he was all finished was priceless.

I have a friend who has been helping refugee families for a couple years. She and her husband arranged, sacrificially, to have the two teenage children in their current family attend a youth church camp. She planned and gave up some of her own money and prayed and poured out, and then told me stories of their amazing experiences with happy tears in her eyes.

I have another friend who gives her time away to women who are hurting. She opens her home and she listens and offers Scripture and words of wisdom and grace and gentleness and prayer. She takes what God has done in her life through many difficult circumstances and pours it all out into other women and, being one of those hurting women, I can attest to the fact that she does not seem empty and tired when we've finished our time together. She seems just as full of the Spirit, if not more, then when I walked into the room.

You know, it's occurring to me - in watching these lives and many more - that when you pour yourself out for someone else, you don't end up completely drained and depleted. You simply, supernaturally, have more room for God to fill you up with blessings and joy and more of Himself.

So, pour and be filled.

Eighty

A Boy, A Ball, and God

A few things have converged in my 12-year-old son's life over the past couple months. Back in the spring, he and I began reading <u>Take Your Best Shot</u> by then-nine-year-old Austin Gutwein, the story of a boy who decided he didn't want to wait until he was all grown up to do something big for God.

Then Jack decided he wanted to attend a Christian school and after a few months of praying and investigating, we moved forward with that decision. In doing so, I found out that Jack would have assignments to complete before school started up again. Yee-haw. I'm such a fan of homework. Let alone *summer* homework. But part of his homework is to read a book called <u>Just Like Jesus</u> by Max Lucado - and write a detailed book report on it - and it's been needling both of us, albeit in very different ways. Today's reading was Mr. Lucado's take on what the leper must've felt who was healed by Jesus. Jack wrote that it reminded him of being at Feed My Starving Children earlier that day.

Jack went with some friends for a packing session today, where they packed meals for children in third-world countries. While we were reading tonight <u>Just Like Jesus</u>, he said, "Did you know that for only ten dollars, you could feed two children for a month?" "I didn't know that, bud... that's amazing," I said.

And then I could tell his mind was going. We've been kicking around the idea for months of ways he could use basketball to raise money for Africa, like Austin Gutwein did, and these books and today's packing session all came together for him.

So I prayed with him before putting him to bed and asked Jesus that if he thought this were a good idea, that he would help us be creative and make it happen. When I stopped praying, Jack said, "I think I know how we're supposed to do this." I grabbed a notebook and took down his thoughts. It was pretty sweet. I pointed out that the Holy Spirit just told him what we should do. I gave him a kiss and told him we'd work on it tomorrow.

He came and got me a few minutes later to show me something. He pointed out what when the light hit the wall across from his bed, the shadows looked like letters. He told me he was asking God to help him see what it said in case it were a message, and before he could tell me, I saw it, "B A L L." "I think it says 'B A L L,'" Jack said. Now, it wasn't like the handwriting on the wall with Daniel or anything, but it was clear enough that I teared up. "Jesus must be trying to encourage you, hon," I said. "I've never had him do that for me before," Jack said with a smile. "Jesus is cool that way, baby," I said as I walked back out, with my own big smile.

Jack came back out a couple minutes later. "I think it maybe also says 'F A I L,'" he said, looking dejected. "Jack, which word do you think Jesus would be saying to you right now --- BALL or FAIL?" "Ball," he answered. "Then we're going with that," I said reassuring him.

The lessons here are many and deep, but I'll just point out a couple. God can speak to us at any time and in any way. Never discount what God wants to do through a child. Always acknowledge a God-thing…I think he loves it when we give him credit. Encouraging our children's very personal walk with God will build their faith and our own. And for heaven's sakes… when the writing on the wall is positive, assume it's from Jesus.

Eighty One

Grown Up

I think I might be growing up. Just a little bit.

I think I'm realizing that the real definition of grown-up is not what I used to think it was. I used to think it meant I would be able to drive or vote or have a martini, all legally. I used to think it meant I could eat what I want when I wanted. (This amuses me to this day when I recall being in my first apartment in college, and getting up in the middle of the night, in my own kitchen by myself, to make myself seven pieces of jelly toast. Talk about exercising my freedom, huh? *Wild woman.*) I used to think it meant the only rules I had to follow were my own. I used to think it meant, basically, I could do whatever I wanted, whenever I wanted, however I wanted.

But that narrow-minded, immature, self-centered definition is being slowly burned away, thankfully. And that narrow-minded, immature, self-centered definition not only does not and has not served me well, but it's gotten me into a heap of trouble more often that I want to admit.

So here's my current definition of being a grown-up: *doing something you don't want to do because it's good for you or someone else.* And not being a big fat whiner about it, I might add.

I must say that I'm not batting a thousand in this area at this moment, but…but I am opening up to this concept more and more. I'm seeing that doing things that are good for you and good for others is obedience. It's transformational. It's putting the action first and trusting that the feeling will follow, at least someday. It's stretching and challenging and, at some point you realize, rewarding and liberating all at the same time.

Part of me is fighting this whole growing up thing, because man, do I like my way, and boy, do I think I know best (for me and pretty much everyone else). But just saying the prayer, "Lord, help me be willing to want what you want…" can open up floodgates in the heavenlies that will bring about untold blessings not just for the person that I seek to touch but also for me, as long as I'm open to them.

"In a word, what I'm saying is, Grow up. You're kingdom subjects. Now live like it. Live out your God-created identity. Live generously and graciously toward others, the way God lives toward you." -Matthew 5:48- (Msg)

Eighty Two

Lay it Down

I've been at two women's events lately that have stirred something up in me. One was a MOPS' group that I was speaking at and one was a retreat that I attended.

At the MOPS' group, I offer to be a listening ear to the girls, mentioning that sometimes it can be freeing to lay your burden at the foot of a stranger and walk away a bit lighter. I had three women come up to my book table at the end of my talk and share deeply troubling life situations. Like, gut-wrenching things. I had been sick that morning, I was a tad medicated, and I had been planning on staying for maybe ten minutes at my table so I could get home and go back to bed. Also, keep in mind, I'm carrying my own heavy burden these days. But Jesus had other plans for me than a nap. I listened to each one as attentively as I could. In my mind I was praying, "Lord, I've got nothing for this woman! Speak through me, please." And then I laid a gentle hand on each one and prayed for her, hoping whatever words the Spirit would bring to my mind would be just what these women needed to hear.

I got in my car, and said to Jesus, "Well, that was just too much." And then I cried for a few minutes. I felt so inadequate and I felt so heavy-hearted because I knew that in that room of fifty women, only three had the courage to come talk to me. Most of the women probably could have lined up and shared a story and needed prayer. Women are hurting.

Then just yesterday I was able to attend a fabulous retreat at a local church and get poured into, and it was just what I needed. After our first session, which focused on weariness, our table discussion leader asked, "What is making you weary these days?" I debated whether to share my burden, even in slivers, to this group of strangers, and even if to fill any awkward silence. I was at a table of ten women…I should have known there'd be no awkward silences. Four of the women shared. And these were not little things. The care of two elderly parents, one with dementia who lives with her and walks around her house at night. One with a fifteen-year-old who has some learning disabilities that are weighing on the entire family. One with a thirty-something son who has moved back in with no purpose and a potential addiction. One with a daughter who has lost hope in life. And there were the other six of us who hadn't had a chance to share. And then I looked around the room and saw the other five hundred or so women and again felt this burden. Women are tired.

Here's what I think God is trying to kindly fit into my head. There are burdens that look nothing like mine and they are equally painful. Pain is pain is pain. And I'm not the only one with a big thing. I would bet that a majority of the women who walked through the doors to both of those events are carrying something around that feels larger than they can handle.

We've all heard it said that "God won't give us more than we can handle". People who think this way claim that this idea is taught in 1 Corinthians 10:13, but what this verse actually says though is that God will not allow you to encounter any temptation to sin without also providing a way for you to avoid it. But does God allow his people to be burdened beyond what they're able to bear? Paul wrote these words, "We were under great pressure, far beyond our ability to endure, so that we despaired even of life." (1 Corinthians 1:9) So, news flash, we *will* be given, from time to time, more than we can handle when it comes to trials and life difficulties. And if you think about it, of course we would. If we could handle everything thrown our way, we wouldn't ever need to call on God's help.

So, if you're burdened, bring your burden to God and allow him to fill you back up and carry it with you. And if you know someone who is, come alongside them in prayer, in compassion, and with hope.

Eighty Three

Water & Fire

I'm attempting to memorize Scripture again. I go in phases. I tell myself I suck at it. But then, I kind of write a verse down on an index card and put it by my kitchen sink and two days later, I realize that I've put another verse to memory. Which is, in my opinion, one of the best spiritual disciplines we can ever put into place.

So, here's yesterday's passage, from Isaiah 43:2-3, from memory, no less:

When you pass through the waters,
I will be with you;
And when you pass through the rivers,
they will not sweep over you.
When you walk through the fire,
you will not be burned,
the flames will not set you ablaze,
for I am the Lord your God.

This passage scares the crud out of me and completely comforts me all at the same time. Here's why. It's full of promises...just not fun promises. Notice all the "whens" instead of the "ifs". We will pass through waters, we will pass through rivers, and we will walk through fires. Oh, yay! Awesome!

But here are the deep reassurances that sink into my soul and calm me down when I let them...God will be with us. The rivers won't make us drown. Not only will we not be burned up, we won't even be touched by the fire surrounding us. And the best peace offering of all --- he who will walk with us is the Lord, and that Lord is our God.

I'm breathing in deeply right now, eyes closed, picturing how these words have played out in my life in the past, how they are now, and how they will when the water and fire comes again. And I can rest assured…I will not drown, I will not be burned. My Lord is with me.

Eighty Four

Twenty-Five

I'm not a theologian. I can't explain all the mysteries of God, why he allows evil in the world, when the end of time is going to happen specifically, things like that. (Then again, I don't know anyone who can...) But I've heard it said that though people may try to refute my faith with scientific or philosophical arguments (these are typically people who don't realize how much archaeological and historical evidence there is that backs up the Christian faith, by the way), no one can argue with my story.

And so this is my story. When I was fifteen, I wrote a prayer to God. I told him that I loved him and I believed in him and I was sorry that I never really read the Bible because I always got stuck towards the end of the book of Genesis but that I would try a lot harder to be a better person. When I was fifteen, I believed that God existed beyond a shadow of a doubt. (Side note: I have never understood how someone can not believe there is a Creator God when they see snow or the sun rise or the ocean or flowers coming back to life in Spring or billions of stars on a clear night...all of that is enough for me to believe in God.) When I was fifteen, I believed that Jesus Christ was God's Son and died on a cross to save our sins.

When I was fifteen, I was a goody goody, through and through. Okay, I had tried a cigarette and a beer. And I had kissed a boy...or three. (For like a sum total of sixty seconds.) I had hidden my vitamins from my mom and told her I had taken them every morning. And that's maybe it. (I'm kidding. But I'm kinda not.) My sin pile was small in my estimation and I was totally sure I would be going to heaven because I was a good girl and I believed in God. I grounded myself for goodness' sakes. Seriously.

But twenty-five years ago, on this day, my world was turned upside down by Truth. I was invited to a place called the Christian Youth Center. I was told there'd be cute boys. That's all this shy girl from a tiny high school needed to hear. Oh, but my Heavenly Father had a totally different plan in mind for me that night.

Because that night – Tuesday, February 4, 1986 – I was told, gently, that I was right in everything I believed except for one important detail. Jesus didn't die for the sins of the world. He died for mine. I had enough sin for him to have to die. I was blown away by this piece of information, and didn't question it for a moment. *Do you want to go to heaven when you die?* I was asked. *Yes!*, I whispered. I was breathless. I knew something huge was happening…I could tell that what I was doing was not just life-changing but eternity-shaping…I could feel it in my bones. I was led through what is called the Sinner's Prayer. Basically, I told God I was a sinner, that I was so sorry, that I believed in him and what his Son did for me on the cross, and then I asked Jesus to come into my heart and be my Lord and Savior. (We now say Leader and Forgiver. All those things are true. He is all of those things and so much more.)

I've told this story who knows how many times and I'm sitting here with tears in my eyes. Because that night was just the beginning of my story. I have lived twenty-five of my forty years trying to follow Jesus. Sometimes running hard and fast after him, sometimes so ashamed at the sin in my life that I could barely look him in the spiritual eyes. Most times though, you'll find me clinging to him for all I'm worth.

I look at people who choose not to live their lives with a spiritual component. Who just have jobs and families and friends and hobbies. And I get all that --- I love all that. Just plain regular life can be really, really good. But I'm amazed. I'm amazed that the void in their souls doesn't drive them to look for God until they find him. I almost can't put words to it, but I cannot imagine living my life without Jesus. Not just sprinkling Jesus on top. Not just praying before meals or on icy roads. Not just weekly church or Christian music.

But a life without Jesus as my absolute Best Friend would be so barren, so desperate. I would be missing out on so much and perhaps not even know it. I talk to him all the time. He is my everything. I love him so much I can hardly stand it sometimes. He not only washes my sin away. He heals me. He prays for me. He thinks I'm amazing. He loves me. He holds me. He speaks to me through his Word in ridiculously intimate ways.

You can say what you want about people who believe in God…you can say we're crazy or flakes or use God as a crutch because we're weak…you can throw whatever scientific equation or philosophical argument at me that you want…but I don't just believe in God. I *know* God. I don't just believe in Jesus. I *know* Jesus. I don't just believe in the Holy Spirit. I *know* the Holy Spirit. They are my life and my breath and today I celebrate with everything in me twenty-five absolutely amazing years walking beside my Creator. I would be nothing without him.

Eighty Five

Broken Things

Though I wouldn't have said this outloud, had someone asked me what set me apart in the Kingdom of God, say, twenty five years ago, I would've believed deep down that I was the poster child for a goody-two-shoes coming to Jesus, and how he could take some gifts and maybe make them a bit better. That was the extent of where I thought my life was headed, the tiny breadth of all I had to offer him.

Fast forward to present day. I'm a little wiser. A little more humble. A little more accurate in my self-perceptions. A lot more banged-up. So now my answer would be this: I'm the poster child for brokenness and, *hopefully*, for beauty coming through despite it all.

I say that with my head held high, not embarrassed or ashamed. Singer/songwriter Kim Hill says it perfectly: *"She's finally seen the light... that he loves broken things...so let all the pieces fall...and see what that freedom brings..."*

There is a freedom in looking your own brokenness in the eye, dragging it out into the light, welcoming it as part of who you are, then handing it all to Jesus and asking him to put the pieces back together and to make something beautiful out of it.

Right now, that's what my life is all about. In all honestly, I'm a bit weary as this is an arduous task. I'm a bit raw, as it takes a lot of time for deep wounds to heal.

But something surprising is happening in me. Though I have always believed that Jesus loves me, and one of my life joys is to remind people that they, too, are loved completely by God, I seem to be understanding his mercy and grace in new ways. Things are being stripped away, and

I'm experiencing a quiet, deep, pervasive, gentle, not-going-anywhere-no-matter-what kind of love that I maybe hadn't been privileged to feel before, at least not in the way I have been. And I am so, so grateful.

I know I sent Jesus to the Cross with my sin...that has been very apparent to me lately, but my soul is being reminded that he went willingly and in doing so, he covers all of what's broken inside me.

So here's to you if you're weary and broken today...here is your word of promise from God, from Psalm 34:18 (NLT):

The LORD is close to the brokenhearted; he rescues those whose spirits are crushed.

Epilogue

That was a hard stretch. I knew it was hard as I was slogging through it and I know it was hard looking back. But I have to say, what a cool experience to see myself trying to be stronger than I was by tapping into the strength and grace of God.

I don't know what your life looks like right now…but I hope and pray that my stories will encourage you to find a way to inspire someone else, serve someone else, love someone else, even if you're hurting. I promise that God will honor that with a blessing, and I promise that he will meet you at the corner of broken and love.

CPSIA information can be obtained
at www.ICGtesting.com
Printed in the USA
FFOW02n0614300414
5155FF

9 781449 722609